NOV - - 2015

Nose,
Legs,
Body!

Len Napolitano

Wineology Press
Templeton, CA

Nose, Legs, Body!

Know Wine
Like The Back of Your Hand

ISBN: 978-0-9893087-0-0
Library of Congress Control Number: 2013942178
Wineology® is a trademark of Len Napolitano
Cover Design: Colin Young
Edited by Diane Browning
Book blog: noselegsbody.com
For information about special discounts for bulk purchases, contact Wineology Press at info@wineology.com
All information in this book is true and complete to the best of our knowledge. Suggestions and exercises are made without guarantee on the part of the author or Wineology Press. The author and publisher disclaim any liability in connection with the use of this information.

Wine can have a negative effect on your reflexes, quality of work, and concentration. Just as winemaking staff, professional wine critics, and competition judges take a sample of wine, hold it in the mouth for a few seconds, and then spit out the wine into a separate container or sink, readers should taste and spit wine when doing the exercises in this book to lessen the chance that mental or physical abilities will be impaired.

WP
Wineology Press
PO Box 1771
Templeton, CA 93465
wineology.com
Published in the United States of America
First printing June 2013

To everyone who has ever asked a question about wine.

Table of Contents

Smells like dirt!

Embracing the Origins of Wine Aroma, Flavor, and Color

1. How does wine get so many flavors and aromas?
2. How does wine get color?
3. What makes chardonnay, or any wine, taste different among producers?
4. Why are some wines blended?
5. Why are some wines filtered?
6. Why is wine aged in oak?

We have three vines in our backyard and make a case of wine every year.

Respecting the Land, Air, and Sun Inside Your Wine

7. What is a wine appellation of origin?
8. What is a vineyard-designated wine?
9. What is terroir?
10. What is the relationship between wine and weather?
11. What is hang time?
12. What can be learned from a visit to a winery?
13. What's happening at a winery during harvest?

Red wine gives me a headache.

Gathering Wine Consumer Intelligence

14. Do sulfites in wine give me a headache?
15. What is organic wine?
16. What is tannin?
17. Why do some dry wines taste sweet?
18. What is a "hot" wine?
19. What should I look for on a wine label?

Preface

Although you don't need intimate knowledge of wine in order to enjoy it, there is no doubt in my mind some wine experiences are enhanced if you have an appreciation for the fundamentals. For instance, if you've ever had the opportunity to taste a significantly aged vintage wine, it could be said you experienced a form of time travel: you consumed a one-of-a-kind product made under the peculiar weather conditions in that particular year, from grapes planted, maintained, harvested, handled, and processed decades earlier by individuals you never knew and possibly are even no longer living. But their wine touched you personally and was very much alive the minute the bottle was opened: long trapped inside a nearly air-tight bottle, it transformed by-the-minute in your glass.

Some fundamental knowledge of wine certainly would have served me well during my first encounter with wine sediment. While sitting with friends and family, I was gazing at a delicate, 25-year-old bottle of red wine moments after it had been slowly and carefully uncorked and placed gently on the table. I was surprised when I noticed tiny black particles floating inside the wine. So, I calmly reached across the table, took the bottle, and started shaking it—as if it were a half-gallon jug of orange juice! I thought if I got the solid bits inside circulating (I probably called it pulp) they would mix with the wine, which would taste better as a result. I was only able to complete one or two shakes of the bottle before others at the table frantically jumped out of their seats, grabbed my arm, and screamed, "No! Put the bottle down!" At the time this occurred, my wine knowledge amounted to little more than how to use a corkscrew. Six years later, the first edition of my weekly wine column, which would run for ten more years in the same newspaper, was published.

My journey from wine-ignorant to wine-intelligent, however, started before I learned about wine sediment. Its unofficial launch was on the day I stopped ordering my usual iced tea with lemon alongside my meal and, instead, asked for the wine list. It was a giant leap of faith: wine list in hand, eager to order a bottle, absolutely no knowledge about wine.

As requesting the wine list grew comfortable over time, a realization of my wine ignorance caused stress every time I actually *held* one. Attempting to decipher it was like trying to read a foreign language of which I knew little more than "hello" and "thank you." Adding to my discomfort was a desire not to pay a lot for wine. Sommeliers (wine experts at restaurants) were usually available to assist, but they intimidated me. I was more comfortable making my own decisions.

But my wine anxiety returned each time I opened the list, perused dozens, if not hundreds of wines, and took shots in the dark at names barely pronounceable. Before long, I was uneasy even asking for the list. That's when I knew a simple and cost-effective method for selecting a bottle with my meal was needed. So, I devised the "cheapest-plus-two" system. It worked like this: search for the lowest-priced wine on the list, move up two price points and *point to that wine*—regardless of wine color, origin, style, or brand—or what I had chosen for my meal!

A self-conscious amateur, I figured if I ordered the cheapest wine I looked like a stingy S.O.B., and if I picked the second-cheapest wine, it was obvious I was disguising a tightwad persona, albeit a false one. Since spending indiscriminately on wine went against my nature, I thought the "cheapest-plus-two" system not only hid my confusion, frustration, and lack of sophistication about wine, it also didn't make me look (too) cheap. Choosing a wine was now fast, easy, and economical.

But implementing "the system" without a basic understanding of wine did not feel right. Having an engineering degree, it bothered me to guess when faced with a decision. To ease my burden, I reminded myself it wasn't like I designed a house, found the cheapest material for the rafters, then jumped two materials up to not look cheap. Fortunately, nothing nearly as serious as a collapsed roof would happen by picking "the wrong wine." But I feared sooner or later a wine-selection disaster would come and I imagined uncontrollable laughter from a waiter the moment I uttered my wine selection with dinner:

Me: "As for the wine, please bring a bottle of the 1985 Chateau...."

Waiter: "Ha-ha-ha-ha-ha-ha-ha! Wait—seriously? With that dish? Ha-ha-ha-ha-ha!

As it turned out, the only thing obvious was the failure of my system to stop fine-dining nightmares in my head. So, I stopped playing wine roulette and obeyed a calling to understand and know wine: I was thirty-something, married, making a decent salary just minutes outside of New York City. I wore a suit to work, for Pete's sake! I shouldn't be sipping iced tea with a fine steak au poivre! I could no longer ignore the voice inside me shouting, "Know wine!"

So I set out to learn—a painfully slow process because most wine books then were inches thick, written by seventy-five-year-old British writers who seemed to take pride in their excessively-detailed maps of France and cared little about American wine. Later, I started taking wine classes, which made learning fun, not to mention fast, compared to those coffee-table-sized books. As learning progressed, I became convinced the age at which one starts out to learn about wine matters little. (I was almost 40.) What matters more is how you learn wine. You can't depend solely on reading wine texts. You need to also see and hear a human "show and tell" it. There is a lot of nuance in wine, both on the palate and in the details of making it—hard to convey in a book alone. Classes are essential to understanding wine. You learn by seeing, smelling, feeling, and tasting wine while simultaneously engaging in discussion on its origin, style, aromas, flavors, finish, texture, and processing. Eventually, you even study excessively-detailed maps of France—and enjoy every minute of it!

When I moved to California, I lived within a couple hours' drive of California's Central Coast wineries. Before long, I was stepping inside winemaking facilities, walking in vineyards, holding clusters of grapes, and smelling the sweet fragrance of fermenting grape juice. Wine was at last being experienced "hands-on." After earning wine-knowledge certification from two organizations, I was the "go-to" person for any question about wine among friends and family and was completely sympathetic to their frustration and desire for clear explanations. They appreciated simple, straightforward answers without intimidating wine-snob lingo. I realized I was able to do this because one half of me, with the engineering background, is accustomed to giving and listening to technical information, while my creative half rejects complication, preferring brevity and clarity. That's when I thought about creating a wine column specifically for people who want simple answers to their questions about wine.

My idea was to take wine questions people have asked, write pithy answers, and turn them into a weekly wine column with an educational approach. I proposed the idea to the Food Section Editor at the *Ventura County Star*, which covered Southern California's Ventura County and northern Los Angeles County. I submitted a few sample questions and answers, named the column "Wineology: Intelligence for the Wine Consumer," and, to my surprise, was accepted and welcomed to the paper. Then, with the help of one of the fine restaurants nearby, I organized and led classes covering the basics of wine and used questions raised during classes to form new wine columns. I held classes at local wine shops, too, while a second publication, *Wine Country This Week* magazine, was added. Within two years, Wineology was not only a wine column, but a road show, too.

This book compiles ten years of wine column and wine class questions from eager beginners, followed by concise answers and useful information. I hope they inspire you to explore further, or maybe even help others discover and appreciate the pleasures of wine. I pray, however, that after you read *Nose, Legs, Body!* you will never apply anything resembling my "cheapest-plus-two" system. I expect you will know wine well enough to decline the wine list altogether and directly inform your server: "I'll have a full-bodied, California, Bordeaux-style red blend, from either the Rutherford or Stag's Leap appellation please, containing not less than 50% cabernet—and not over-oaked!—but with silky tannins to pair with my steak au poivre."

The wine won't be anywhere near the cheapest on the list, but I promise it will create an infinitely more enjoyable dining experience than iced tea with lemon. More important, it won't start the waiter laughing. (Then again, maybe it will.)

Introduction

Wine is both simple and complex. The simple side of the story says grapes grow wild, ripen, mix with yeasts, and ferment; juice miraculously turns into wine. But wine has a terribly complex side, too. For example, I don't envy winemakers faced with questions about how much sulfite will preserve a wine, whether fruit acids should be added, and when to do it; how to manage wine pH that is outside the normal range or a fermentation that suddenly stops and won't restart; whether to add enzymes, what type of yeast to use, or whether to reduce alcohol content. Thankfully, for me at least, these and similarly tough questions are not addressed in this book. Rather, it aims to satisfy the curious wine novice who wonders, for example, *why* wine is aged in oak, *not* what species of oak was used, in which forest the tree was grown, or the temperature range at which the oak barrel was exposed to an open flame—all questions, by the way, for which a thinking winemaker will want answers.

While peppered with personal stories, this book is centered on the questions people have asked me about wine. Rounded down to a neat 50, they cover subjects critical to building a firm foundation of wine knowledge. Each question is answered first in a nutshell, and then followed by a more detailed, though not comprehensive explanation. On a subject as broad and diverse as wine, a writer could take any one of the questions and write an entire volume answering it—and some have! So, in keeping with a culture of texts and tweets, this book delivers wine knowledge to you in succinct packets of information.

The questions and answers in the book are arranged by subjects that form natural chapter themes. They are:

- the composition of wine
- the vineyard, the weather, and the winery
- wine myths and modern day issues
- styles of wine
- enjoying wine with food
- appreciating fine wine as a lifestyle

Each chapter theme can be reinforced with simple wine exercises to do at home, contained in a concluding sidebar, "Know It Like the Back of Your Hand." Chapter titles, by the way, are verbatim statements made by friends or wine class attendees. They do for chapter themes what aroma does for wine: they tease.

Wine terms commonly used among enthusiasts and professionals are indicated with **boldface** font and defined within the context of the chapter and in the Glossary of Terms. The book contains six appendices providing more information and quick-reference tables on a variety of subjects discussed in the book. Finally, a list of links to wine resources mentioned in the book can be found in the Resources section and also on the "Ebook Links" page of the book's blog, noselegsbody.com.

Same Grape, Different results.

**Three Reasons Why Wines
Made From The Same Grape Variety
Vary Among Producers**

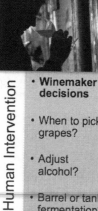

Location

- **Growing Conditions**

- Warm or cool?

- Rainy or dry?

- Mostly fog or clear?

- Type of soil

- Topography & elevation

Human Intervention

- **Winemaker decisions**

- When to pick grapes?

- Adjust alcohol?

- Barrel or tank fermentation?

- Percentage of new oak barrels?

- How long to age wine?

- Should wine be blended?

- Should wine be filtered?

Time

- **Vintage**

- Is the wine young or mature?

Chapter 1

Smells like dirt!

Embracing the Origins of Wine Aroma, Flavor and Color

At precisely 5PM on a Friday, at the door leading to a back room of a popular Los Angeles wine store, enthusiastic wine tasters, from beginner to expert, pay a nominal fee to experience a handful of world famous wines. Within minutes, a two-ounce sample of a very pricey French luxury wine is poured for every man and woman squeezed three-deep against the bar. Then, in seemingly simultaneous motion, noses all around plunge deep inside glasses and a buzz of praise sweeps across the room as millions of microscopic molecules of seductive volatile odorants—*smell*—make their way to dozens of olfactory receptors—*noses*. I turn to the person next to me, who I happen to know falls into the wine novice category, and ask for the first thing that comes to her mind after she takes her first sniff. "Smells like dirt!," she exclaims. Not what I expected to hear, but a perfectly legitimate assessment.

Most of what we taste and appreciate in wine stems from its aroma. If you hold your nose as you sip wine, you will taste little, if anything at all. Even as wine is held inside your mouth, its aroma continues to expand as body heat raises the wine's temperature. It travels through a passageway in the back of the throat that leads to nasal receptors. With each sniff and sip, additional wine components excite the tongue, sensing flavor, sweetness, acidity, bitterness, sourness, or texture. But aroma alone forms your first—and often a lasting—impression.

Exclaiming a wine smells like dirt may be reasonable and appropriate, but a wine industry person probably would use terms like "earthy" or "damp soil." After a little more thought, my friend might have applied more refined words to describe her wine, but she had already, unknowingly, scored high on wine appreciation's Instant Lesson One: *say what you think you smell; find the "right" words later.*

Each wine appreciation class I conducted over the past decade began with everyone smelling a sample of a wine, but I didn't disclose any information about it—not the type of wine, the producer, region, or even the state of origin. I asked everyone to write down words that described what they were smelling and to keep their notes to themselves. Then, I invited them to shout out their descriptors as I wrote them on a board for everyone to see.

Next, they took a minute to take a sip of the wine and shouted words that described what they tasted. As each person randomly called out a descriptor, and I posted it on the board, I always saw others discovering that they also tasted, or smelled, the same thing—but realizing it only after someone else said it. This phenomenon became Instant Lesson Two: *when tasting a wine, help yourself identify what you smell and taste with a prepared list of potential wine aromas and flavors.* (See the quick-reference table in Appendix 5.)

The next step made the lesson more interesting. I read aloud a description of the wine, *as it was written and published by the producer*—often from the winemaker's own tasting notes. Here's an example, using Sonoma County, California's Dry Creek Vineyard 2009 proprietary blend, The Mariner:

> *The 2009 Mariner presents enticing aromas with deep vibrant hues of attractive red fruits. Aromas are dominated by cassis and dark cherry, toasted vanilla oak, hints of crème brûlée and notes of espresso. On the palate, the*

flavors are harmonious and supple with blackberry and sweet black cherry combining with a toasty complexity. The tannins are fine and grainy, lending excellent structure to this wine. The finish is long and lingering with a charming flavor profile that entices one for another sip.

We then compared the winery's description of the wine to the aromas and flavors on the board. Some words were identical matches with words shouted by class members. Others were different from, and sometimes contradictory to, the winery's notes. But my objective wasn't to get matches. I wanted people to know Instant Lesson Three: *there are no absolute right answers to tasting wine; what each of us senses is unique and personal.* Only you know what you smell and taste (and whether or not it is pleasing). It is not uncommon for one person to be certain she tastes blueberry, for example, while another gets nothing remotely resembling it. This brought relief to many in the class. For them, it was their first victory in an effort to conquer wine's mystique.

But the final and most fun step was still to come. This was the part I looked forward to most. I led the class in what I called a "reverse" wine tasting. I poured for each person samples of four wines—two red, two white—and numbered them one through four. Again, I revealed nothing. I invited everyone to take time to smell and taste all four wines, taking notes on the aromas, flavors, and any other characteristics, positive or negative. After everyone finished tasting and writing, I read out loud the winery's description of each of the four wines they just tasted—but I identified the descriptions as A through D (not one through four), and I read them in random order. I asked the class to refer to their notes and correlate each lettered description with one of the four numbered wines. In other words, they had to match each wine's number to the lettered description they felt best applied to the wine. Not only was reading the winemaker's tasting notes great exposure to industry lingo for the class, it forced non-linear thinking and supplemented the aroma-flavor learning process.

Agreement over what a wine delivers to the senses is never unanimous, as these exercises demonstrated when a group of people tastes the same wine. Even a group of wine professionals judging a wine competition disagree. Getting *a majority* of people to agree, however, is not impossible. It becomes easier when there are triggers—in this case, the shouted words and winemaker's notes—helping tasters identify aromas and flavors. Whether or not that same majority thinks the wine is any good is another question.

Thus, describing the aroma of a wine as reminiscent of dirt is as good a start as any for discussion about the composition of wine. As for my wine appreciation classes—a roomful of people shouting out names of fruits, spices, minerals, flowers, vegetables, animals, and other sensory delights—invariably the ultimate pressing question emerged:

How did all these aromas and flavors get inside the wine?

1. How does wine get so many flavors and aromas?

The single biggest source of what you smell and taste in a wine is the grape. Naturally formed chemical compounds on the surface of the skin and within its juice produce enticing fragrance and a variety of flavors. A secondary source is the oak barrel in which a wine was aged.

Each type of grape, also referred to as a grape variety—from chardonnay to zinfandel—gets its primary flavors as it grows on the vine; it creates a "default" flavor profile based on the grape's genetic composition. This primary flavor profile forms the grape's **true varietal character**. For example, you may have noticed flavors and aromas similar to melon and tropical fruit in virtually every chardonnay; blackcurrant and cassis in cabernet sauvignon; red and black cherry in pinot noir. Although there are always variations in degree, these characteristics are fairly typical of wines made from these grapes regardless of where the wine is made or who makes it. True varietal character develops as the grapevine, like all plants, converts sunlight energy to chemical activity in the natural process of **photosynthesis.**

Yeast, a microscopic organism living on grape skins, gets to work releasing true varietal character—and creating even more flavors—once thousands of grapes have been picked from vines, cracked open, and transferred to a tank or bin. As sugar in the grapes is converted into alcohol by yeast, sweet fresh juice evolves into dry, potent wine. Later, even more wine flavors and aromas emerge during the wine's aging period when chemical compounds interact with each other and microscopic amounts of air. Generally, fragrance developed during aging is referred to as wine **bouquet**, while "aroma" derives *directly from fermentation.*

Wines aged in oak barrels get additional contributions of aroma and flavor from wood, variable due to differences in both the geographic origin of the tree (most often, America or France) and the degree to which the wood is **toasted** (heated by exposure to an open flame). Toasted oak can add hints of coconut, vanilla, mocha, coffee, toasted bread, or clove, among other aspects, while injecting sweetness to the wine's bouquet. Brand new barrels filled with wine for the first time add these qualities with significantly greater impact than older barrels. Old, aroma-less barrels, referred to as neutral, are used to hold wine during aging *without adding new flavors.*

While primary flavors and aromas originate from grapes, specifically, it's the grape skin that gives color to wine...

2. How does wine get color?

The juice inside both white and red grapes is virtually clear. Juice gets color as pigments on grape skins are extracted into the juice and it continues to darken the longer skins and juice stay in physical contact. Also, some red grape varieties with darker pigmentation produce more deeply colored wines, while varieties with naturally small berries have increased skin-to-juice ratio, adding intensity to wine color.

While the range of colors and shades of white wine, rosé wine, and red wine span from pale yellow, to pink, to deep purple, how each type achieves color is dependent partly upon the grape variety, the size of the grape berry, and the exposure to oxygen of the juice, but mostly on the duration of the juice-to-skin contact.

Though seldom done, it is possible to make white wine from red grapes, but red wine can only be made from red grapes. In red winemaking, colorless juice is released as red grapes are crushed and then pumped into a stainless steel tank or plastic bin. As skins break open, color pigments in the skins make contact with the juice; juice darkens and gets more intense color with longer skin contact. This skin-and-juice contact period, called **maceration**, or **cold-soaking**, could last from a few hours to a couple of weeks, depending on the wine and winemaker's preferences.

At some point during maceration, the fermentation process may start, either by natural yeast, or through the winemaker's manual addition of a commercially-packaged, **cultured yeast**. Fermentation is visibly evident from a bubbling surface of the juice caused by the release of carbon dioxide gas and heat as sugar converts to alcohol. The gas pressure inside this dense mixture of juice, grape pulp, skins, seeds and stems, called **must**, causes the solids to rise to the top. And the biggest contributor to color—grape skins—is trapped within this top layer of solids as the relatively clear juice stays below it—not good if you want red wine to actually be red.

To extract color, this **cap** of solids has to be manually pushed back into the juice, or **punched down**, to keep the pigment-rich skins in contact with as much juice as possible during maceration and fermentation. When fermentation takes place inside plastic bins or oak barrels that stand upright with one end open, punch-down is done manually several times a day using a long-stemmed, punch-down tool. When juice ferments inside large stainless steel tanks too large to punch down by hand, juice is instead directed from the bottom of the tank through a hose and into a pump, which sends the wine back to the top of the tank. This version of red wine color-extraction process is called a **pump-over**.

Before white wine is fermented, grape juice is separated from the skins as soon as possible by immediately **pressing** the grapes with mechanical force to break them open and then pumping juice away from skins while it is still relatively clear. Even though the skins of white grapes are light green, yellow, or golden, they may still contribute color if left in contact with the juice. Some winemakers extend contact time to extract as much aroma as possible from white grape skins but not long enough to add too much color or increase bitterness. The juice from pressing is then sent into a stainless steel tank and mixed with yeast to start fermentation.

The pressing step is also applied to red winemaking, however it comes *after* fermentation finishes, when virtually all sugar is converted to alcohol. But prior to red wine pressing, an initial volume of **free-run wine** is allowed to gravity-flow freely from its mass of skins and solids. Typically dark purple, it may be a little cloudy, but relatively clean compared to what's left behind.

Pressing red wine squeezes out the last amounts of wine from the leftover, skin-rich mass of solids. This dark, **press wine** is considered lower quality than free-run wine because of its harsher taste, but the extent to which it will be added to lighter free-run wine allows the winemaker to control the intensity of final wine color and texture. After pressing, the dry, cake-like residue of solids, called **pomace**, is tilled back into the soil between rows of vines.

Okay, but what about rosé wine? Is it a blend of white wine and red wine? No, except in the making of pink Champagne, where white wine is added to red wine to create a pale shade of red. But for still rosé wine, i.e., non-sparkling, color comes in one of two ways.

One method allows skin contact with juice for a period only long enough to create a light, pink color. Juice then gets transferred to a separate tank and fermented. The other technique pumps some pale juice from the fermenting must of red wine before punching down and ferments it separately. This latter,"bleeding off" process is called **saignée** (pronounced sahn-yay). Saignée has the added effect of creating a more concentrated, darker-colored must in the tank from which it was bled. This step might be done for that purpose alone and not for making a rosé wine.

Identical grape varieties may have similar flavors, aromas and color, but the end product will have noticeable differences among producers, crafted either by the hands of the winemaker, the earth under the vines, or the climate surrounding it...

3. What makes chardonnay, or any wine, taste different among producers?

Variations in regional climate, differences in vineyard soils, and countless individual choices made by the winemaker create a producer's style. Each factor influences lightness or richness, sweetness or dryness, uniqueness or conformity in the wine—and the overall impression it leaves with you.

There are over 7,500 wineries throughout the U.S. Over one-third of them make chardonnay. Close to half of them—3,437—produce cabernet sauvignon. Makes you wonder, does the country really need that many chardonnays or cabernets? How much can these wines, made from the same grape, differ from one another?

Actually, every one of them is unique.

Why? The foremost reason is climate. Grapes grown in a cool climate retain a higher level of **acidity** than the same grape variety grown in a warm climate. The high acid component produces a crisp freshness on the palate, whereas the warm climate grapes lose most of their acidity but develop more sugar. Higher sugar means higher alcohol potential. Higher alcohol adds weight to the wine, lending an impression of sweetness. Chardonnay, for example, grown in these two disparate environments may produce two very different wine styles. This difference in crispness verses weightiness is a difference in **mouthfeel**, a combination of viscosity with astringency or acidity.

Vineyard soils also influence a wine's flavor profile. Soil types vary greatly throughout California and around the world. Chalk, limestone, clay, sand, gravel, loam, mineral components, or volcanic deposits in soils each make unique contributions to wine. Two examples:

- Grapes grown in the gravel, sand, loam, and volcanic-deposit soils of the Rutherford area of California's Napa Valley are said to produce wines with an identifiable

"Rutherford dust" character, described as a unique herbaceous spiciness.

- The limestone-rich soil of the Chablis region in France is a big reason why chardonnay grapes harvested there produce wines of a steely, flinty quality.

Another factor is how the winemaker applies oak. The use of oak in fermentation or the aging process brings more presence to a wine's mouthfeel, along with sweet flavor and aroma. The greatest impact comes from new oak barrels filled with wine for the first time. So, choose an "un-oaked" chardonnay, for example, if you prefer a crisp, lighter mouthfeel. Conversely, if you like a soft, buttery style with a hint of vanilla, look for chardonnay aged with at least 40% new oak, or made using one or all of these processes:

- **Barrel-fermented**: Chardonnay fermented inside an oak barrel absorbs toasted oak compounds from the barrel as fermentation progresses, mostly adding weight to the wine but also a touch of sweet aroma.
- **Aged-on-the-Lees:** Lees are tiny dead yeast cells that settle at the bottom of a wine barrel, or tank, after fermentation is complete. About every other week during aging, they are manually stirred to mix more with the wine and create a rich, creamy mouthfeel.
- **Malolactic Fermentation:** ML is a secondary fermentation, caused by injecting the wine with a natural lactic acid bacteria that converts tart, apple-like acid into softer, milk-like acid, creating chardonnay with a rounder mouthfeel.

Many choices made by winemakers contribute unique style to a wine, differentiating it from others made with the same grape variety. One decision is whether or not to combine it with wine made from other grapes...

4. Why are some wines blended?

Blending wines made from different grape varieties creates a more interesting finished wine; it improves flavor, aroma, or texture—sometimes all three—and can fill gaps or cover weaknesses of the primary grape.

The term **blend** refers to a wine composed of *two or more different varietal wines*. Technically, even a single-varietal wine is built from a blend of wines: though the wines are made from the same grape variety, they may have come from separate vineyards, fermented with different yeasts, or aged in a variety of barrels. Whether using the same variety or a combination of different ones, blending builds a more interesting wine.

Perhaps the most famous blended red wine in the world is French Bordeaux, a blend of two to five different grapes, frequently including cabernet sauvignon and merlot. Bordeaux's other red "blending grapes" are petit verdot (contributes color and structure), cabernet franc (contributes structure and richness of flavor), and malbec (contributes flavor and some sweetness).

The reason Bordeaux winemakers, among others, blend merlot with cabernet sauvignon is to soften, or round out, cabernet's palate-drying texture. Cabernet can have more aggressive **tannin**, an astringent quality in red wine derived from grape skins, seeds, and stems during maceration and fermentation. Cabernet sauvignon grapes naturally develop more tannin than merlot, so blending them lessens cabernet's rigidity.

There are also red wines made in Bordeaux from a single grape variety, as well as delicious white wine blends made from the sauvignon blanc and sémillon grapes. In the Rhone Valley, another legendary French region, blending a small amount of white wine with red wine makes the aromatic, deeply colored Châteauneuf-du-Pape. It is made from a blend of up to 13 different grape varieties, including syrah, a red grape, and viognier, a white wine grape. Additionally, Australian and American wines have had great success blending syrah with cabernet sauvignon.

The breakdown in percentages of the varieties that make up a blend may be indicated on the label, depending on the country of origin, though it is not required for American wines. In Australia, laws require a bottle's label to show the percentages of each grape that make up the blend, from highest to lowest—quite helpful to the curious consumer.

Finally, when producers in the United States make a blended red wine using the same grapes as a classic Bordeaux-blend wine, they are permitted to identify the wine as **Meritage** (rhymes with heritage), a unique, and legally protected term. It is not allowed on a wine if a non-Bordeaux grape, such as zinfandel or syrah, makes up any part of the blend. *It is still a blended wine*, however not a Meritage blend.

5. Why are some wines filtered?

Filtration removes tiny particles with the potential to create a visible haziness in a wine or impair its aroma or flavor after bottling. Filtration makes wine clearer and brighter, while ensuring a longer, more stable shelf-life.

Arguably, many steps of the winemaking process are clarification steps. For instance, the flow of free-run wine from the solids of fermentation is a clarification step. The separation of chardonnay from the lees, called **racking**, also results in a clearer wine. Racking, the transfer of any wine from one oak barrel or stainless steel tank into another, separates the clearer wine from sediment left behind—just like transferring an old wine with sediment from bottle to decanter.

However, the elaborate automated process of filtration clarifies thousands of gallons of wine at a time—and there are risks. The decision to filter depends upon whether a winemaker believes the process will significantly improve wine clarity, character, and long-term integrity. One school of thought believes aggressive filtering removes beneficial, natural compounds in a wine responsible for its unique flavor, style, strength, and aging potential. So, while not filtering wine opens the possibility that an off-taste might develop in the bottle, filtering too much out of the wine could leave it flat and uninteresting. Most often, even expensive luxury brand wines pass once through a coarse filter, removing only the largest particles, leaving the smallest ones to allow the wine to keep its personality.

While a wine doesn't normally state that it was filtered, those not filtered often proudly announce "Unfiltered" right on the front label. Although it is not an indication of quality in either case, you may want to make a mental note of any red wines you especially enjoy and see if they are unfiltered. It's a winemaking step to be aware of, though not one that should influence your purchasing decision.

Two other clarification processes to know:

- **Fining**: Stabilizes wine by addressing microscopic particles that filtering cannot address, but, if left in the wine might create aroma or flavor faults over time. Fining typically happens around the same time as filtering, to prepare wine for life inside the bottle.
- **Cold Stabilization**: Chills wine to near freezing temperatures to precipitate two chemical compounds— tartrate and bitartrate. Formed naturally during fermentation, these compounds later might settle at the bottom of the bottle or cling to the cork. Without cold stabilization, bottled wine exposed to extreme cold storage conditions could precipitate the tartrates. In the event you open a bottle that contains these tiny, glass-like shards, don't be concerned. Just separate them from the wine using a fine-mesh kitchen strainer.

Along this long road to crafting great wine, perhaps the biggest decision—if not the most expensive one—focuses on the oak barrel, one of the most enchanting symbols in winemaking...

6. Why is wine aged in oak?

Oak's natural fragrance and textural characteristics emerge when the wood is heated. When the heated surface is the inside wall of a wine barrel, these pleasing components integrate with wine, influencing its mouthfeel, aroma, flavor, and overall style.

The practice of aging wine in an oak barrel, now a centuries-old tradition, came about by accident. Long before the mass production of glass bottles, wine was sold in bulk and transported in wooden barrels. Wine merchants in England, the world's largest customer of French wine at the time, purchased and resold it by the barrel.

In the course of storing wine in barrels and transporting it across the English Channel, small changes happened: aroma improved, flavor sweetened, and mouthfeel amplified. Also evident, the wine lasted longer. Changes like these didn't go unnoticed by merchants and producers who concluded that the weeks and months wine spent in contact with wood enhanced and preserved it. The benefits of wood contact with wine eventually became part of their normal winemaking regimen.

Oak became the material of choice over other woods because of its abundance, inherent characteristics of hardness and durability, and its ease in bending when heated. It also has good anti-leaking properties, despite allowing microscopic amounts of air to pass through without spoiling the wine—an added benefit responsible for the graceful aging of wine.

Perhaps oak's most important contribution is flavor. If you ever get a chance to watch an oak barrel being made, the wood's potential for flavor is immediately obvious as soon as the wood is heated by an open flame. This **toasting** process extracts natural aroma compounds, smelling as sweet as a cake baking in an oven. Sweetness, like vanilla and mocha, are among many aromatic and flavor contributions of toasted oak. Others are almond, clove, nutmeg, exotic spice, and char, each of which has potential to complement certain wines. Depending on the level of aroma desired, the toasting process lasts anywhere from 15 minutes to around 45 minutes.

When balanced with wine's other components, and under the guidance of a skilled winemaker, seamless integration of wine and wood can create irresistible results. A problem might come if the impact from oak in the wine overtakes the fruit flavor of the grape. When true varietal character is overwhelmed by oakiness, pairing with food becomes more difficult.

Red wines almost always aged in oak include cabernet sauvignon, merlot, zinfandel, syrah, pinot noir, and sangiovese. The most popular white wine to age in barrels is chardonnay, but there are a handful of other white wines that benefit from some oak barrel aging, as well.

Know It Like The Back of Your Hand

Remember, 80% of what you taste in wine comes from its aroma. So, it's important to train your olfactory receptors to recognize potential wine scents. That means taking time to stop and smell the roses! Make it a habit to smell and memorize as many of the wine-related scents listed in Appendix 5. Build your sensory vocabulary. But don't overwhelm your nose in any one session. Rest between sniffs, giving yourself a moment to focus and store each fragrant memory.

Taste wine regularly to build your foundation of wine knowledge. Start by training your palate to know *single-grape varietal wines* before the more complex blended wines. This will help you become familiar with each grape's true varietal character. Depending on how frequently you taste wine, you may want to devote one to two weeks exposing your palate to just one grape variety before moving on to another for the next week or two. Restrict your choices to the wines below, and try to find wines made with 100% of one grape variety.

White: sauvignon blanc, chardonnay

Red: pinot noir, cabernet sauvignon, zinfandel, syrah

Below are exercises designed to develop wine aroma recognition:

- Open jars of spices and jams, sniff inside, and learn to identify the scents without looking. Make it more fun by asking someone to hand you a spice jar as you close your eyes and try to guess which spice it is.
- Smell the scents of flowers and identify them.
- Make the effort to locate and taste less common fruits and spices. Look for blackcurrant, cassis, quince, allspice, and mango. If you can't find the fruit itself, get a jar of jam made from it.
- Purchase a few wines about which people have posted tasting notes on websites, such as CellarTracker.com. Put aside time to taste each wine, take notes on what you smell and taste, and compare your impressions to what others say.
- Learn to distinguish an oak-aged wine from one with no oak component. Do this exercise with chardonnay—it is an easy wine to find in both oaked and un-oaked versions. Try to find a producer, such as Sonoma's Windsor Oaks, that makes chardonnay in both versions.
- Get in the habit of smelling the wine in your glass before your first taste.

Know Wine Math

A typical Napa vineyard acre contains 600 to 1000 vines...

...and yields about 4 tons of grapes per acre

One ton of red grapes makes about 155 gallons of wine

1 vine yields about 10 pounds of grapes

1 bottle of wine is made from about 2-1/2 pounds of grapes

Chapter 2

We have three vines in our backyard and make a case of wine every year.

Respecting the Land, Air, and Sun Inside Your Wine

Here's a fun wine-drinking game to play with friends while visiting wine country: every time you see or hear the phrase, "Our wine is made in the vineyard," or "Great winemaking begins in the vineyard," everyone has to finish the wine in their glass. Make sure you have a designated driver.

If I were to collect a list of clichés about wine, these would top the list. I've seen them in winery slogans, ad headlines, website tag lines, on t-shirts and wine labels. I am tempted to say they have been overused enough to have lost their meaning, but that would be unfair because the statements are absolutely true: it does take a great vineyard to make great wine. I just wish the marketing people found more creative ways to say it.

A wine made from poor quality grapes is hard to sell. There is not much a producer can do other than price it low and adjust it with lots of new oak flavor to cover flaws. Winemakers will always tell you "it's possible to make bad wine from great grapes, but it's not possible to make great wine from bad grapes." (I'll have to add this to my list.)

Almost anywhere in the continental U.S., one can grow grapevines in a backyard and make a case or two of wine each year. When living in Southern California, I created space on my property to grow grapes, but I had to choose them carefully. Although within the northern hemisphere's grape-growing belt, it was still important to select a variety that thrived in Southern California's Mediterranean climate and could produce grapes in my backyard's **microclimate**—the specific weather inherent to my vineyard location, a key factor in shaping a wine's flavor profile.

I planted 22 vines of syrah, chosen for its durability under the high temperature climate in which I lived. Then it was up to me not to mess things up later (and I did). With friends' help picking grapes, and my wife literally stomping grapes with her bare feet, I made several cases of wine in only the vineyard's second year of growth. (A commercial vineyard would wait longer before harvesting grapes for winemaking. Vines start producing a significant volume of quality grapes in the third, and sometimes fourth, growing season.)

Wine is unique among beverages. Its value, both monetary and intrinsic, correlates with the geographic origin of its source material. The same does not apply to beer or whiskey, for example, although one could argue that German beer is different from American or Belgian beer, or that whiskey from the United States is nothing like Scotland's. But, aside from a general connection to a country, *precisely where in the country* the beer or whiskey's barley came from matters little, if at all, to the consumer. There are no differences in barley grown in different regions of the beer- and whiskey-producing countries impacting the value of the product to the same extent that different wine regions around the world impact the value and quality of wine.

What makes wine grapes so special?

It's their need for a defined environment in which they can grow and thrive. There are two narrow bands—one roughly spanning between 30 and 50 degrees latitude north of the equator, and one from 30 to 50 degrees to the south—where all grapes for the fine wines of the world have grown since the first wine-producing grapevines were discovered, some 7000 to 8000 years ago. Interestingly, because seasons of the two hemispheres change in reverse of each other, the grape growing seasons are also opposite. The Northern Hemisphere's vineyards are harvested in early autumn, which is springtime in the Southern Hemisphere, where vineyards in Australia, New Zealand, South America, and South Africa are just starting their growing season. Their autumn harvest coincides with the Northern Hemisphere's early spring. (This makes it possible for ambitious freelance winemakers to work themselves crazy by traveling between hemispheres to work harvest nearly year-round. Knowing the rigors of harvest, I would expect it's the younger winemakers who are more likely to give that a go.)

These narrow growth bands around the globe indicate grapes' sensitivity to their surroundings. And every vineyard location is unique for its own particular template of soil(s), average hours of sunlight, average humidity, annual rainfall and drainage efficiency, day-to-night temperature swings, wind direction and speed, elevation, and proximity to a body of water. Think of it as a vineyard site's DNA.

Even a section within a vineyard, a **vineyard block,** with soil or conditions different from the land immediately surrounding it, can create a unique wine profile. By the same token, the larger vineyard is distinct within the wine region to which it belongs, which stands out from other wine regions in the state, and so on. This is why labels for the wines of all the world's producers indicate the geographic origin of the grapes—sometimes down to the precise vineyard. Beer labels don't. You'll never see or hear the slogan, "Our beer is made in the barley fields!" It just doesn't have the ring of an irresistible cliché.

You may not know it, but you live within a wine-producing region. Your state and your county are "appellations of origin." And if you make wine from your backyard vines, you can print your state or county name on your label. What's more, your case of wine is truly unique because of the singular conditions surrounding those three vines in *your* backyard vineyard. You can tell everyone it's where a great wine begins.

7. What is a wine appellation of origin?

Every wine's grapes have a geographical derivation known as the appellation of origin—the region where the grapes were grown. Appellations vary in size and shape, from an entire country, as with some imported wines; a state; a county; or a specified area as small as a few hundred acres or large enough to cross state borders.

An **appellation of origin** is the geographic region where the grapes for a specific wine were sourced. It is typically a single *state*, or *county*, or up to three counties in the same state. With state and county appellations of origin, defined by governmental boundaries, *at least 75% of the wine comes from grapes grown in the appellation specified on the label.* The two biggest exceptions: the "California" appellation requires 100%; "Texas" requires a minimum of 85%.

Further, a geographic region *not defined by state or county lines* but *possessing distinct climate, geology, soil, topography, and elevation*—features responsible for the distinctive wines made from grapes grown in that area—is entitled to the more prestigious status of **American Viticultural Area (AVA)**. Therefore, an appellation of origin is not necessarily an AVA, but every AVA is a qualified appellation of origin.

For example, Napa Valley—as defined by physical boundaries outlining distinct geology, topography, soil, and elevation—is an approved AVA situated within Napa County, which is defined by governmental county borders. Napa County is not an AVA—but it can be an appellation of origin; similarly, California is an appellation of origin, but it is not an AVA. The U.S. Alcohol and Tobacco Tax and Trade Bureau (TTB) reviews proposals to create AVAs and authorizes their boundaries as official and legal. If an

AVA is specified on a wine label, *at least 85% of the wine's grapes must be grown within that AVA.*

There are 208 AVAs designated throughout the U.S. as of May 2013. California contains 116 AVAs, the first of which was Napa Valley, designated in 1981. However, Napa Valley is the second oldest in the nation. The first official American Viticultural Area— called Augusta, located in…Missouri!—was established in 1980.

An AVA may be created within a larger "parent" AVA, if the smaller area, called a sub-AVA, is distinguished by its own distinct geography and conditions under which distinct wines are made. Again, consider the Napa Valley: there are currently 15 sub-AVAs within the broad Napa Valley AVA. The Stags Leap District, Rutherford, Carneros and the newest, Calistoga, established in 2010, are four examples of sub-AVAs within Napa Valley.

An AVA stated on a label serves as helpful information to wine consumers. Because winemakers and wine enthusiasts understand that unique soils and climate conditions produce unique wines, an AVA designation indicates a certain consistency of style. In addition, as AVAs get sub-divided into smaller AVAs, wine style becomes more focused and consistent. It is significant that a wine from a small AVA is not necessarily of superior quality to a wine harvested from a broader AVA.

There is no minimum size for an area to deserve official AVA status. The smallest one is in California's Mendocino County, called Cole Ranch. At 150 acres, it is smaller than some vineyards! The largest is the Ohio River Valley: it includes parts of the states of Indiana, Kentucky, Ohio, and West Virginia and covers over one million acres. A complete and current list of all AVAs is on the website of the Wine Institute, an advocacy organization for California wine.

In Europe, where the concept of wine appellations began (Hungary actually created the world's first vineyard classification system in 1730), winemakers and grape-growers must adhere to established regulations if they want their wine eligible for "appellation of origin" status on the wine label. Not surprisingly, these wine-growing regions are referred to as controlled appellations, and each wine-producing country in Europe has its own controlling authority. Their official appellation "stamp of approval" is permitted on the label if a producer meets strict grape-growing and winemaking standards. Here are the names of controlling authorities that appear on labels for wines made in Europe's top four wine-producing countries:

France: Appellation d'Origine Contrôlée (AOC)

Italy: Denominazione di Origine Controllata (DOC), and the more stringent Denominazione di Origine Controllata e Garantita (DOCG)

Spain: Denominaciónes de Origen (DO), and the more stringent Denominaciónes de Origen Calificada (DOC)

Germany: Qualitätswein bestimmter Anbaugebiete (QbA), and the more stringent Qualitätswein mit Prädikat (QmP)

Meeting a European appellation's standards typically means not exceeding maximum vineyard yields (grape tons harvested per acre) and not using grapes lacking approval of the authority, among other vineyard and winemaking rules. As we all know, rules are not always followed, like when a French producer makes a wine with non appellation-approved grapes. The wine will get a reduced status of classification, from the prestigious controlled appellation (AOC) class to a more basic, minimally regulated category of **Vin de Pays**, or the even less-stringent category, **Vin de Table**, depending on how far the producer strayed beyond the guidelines.

In 1971, Italian producer Piero Antinori chose not to follow his Tuscan sub-appellation's requirement for every Chianti DOC wine to contain at least 70% sangiovese grapes. Antinori instead made a "Chianti-style" wine, blending some sangiovese with cabernet sauvignon (a Bordeaux grape!). It was wildly successful around the world, and the "modified Chianti" started a new trend in "rogue" Italian wines from Tuscany, unofficially called "Super Tuscans."

Wine-growing regions in Australia, New Zealand, South Africa, Chile, and Argentina are less restricted than European regions and operate closer to the degree at which American wineries are regulated, with minimum percentages required in appellation-designated wines.

Ultimately, a wine appellation doesn't exist without vineyards—in effect, the ultimate "appellation of origin…"

8. What is a vineyard-designated wine?

When a single parcel of land grows grapes of distinction, the wine's producer may choose to include the vineyard name on the label. It indicates a wine of unique character within a given appellation.

More geographically specific than a wine appellation, or even a sub-AVA, is a vineyard of grape origin. Though not by itself an appellation of origin, if a vineyard is indicated on a label, *at least 95% of the grapes must have been grown in that vineyard.*

The producer of a **vineyard-designated**, or **single-vineyard** wine, believes grapes grown there produce a uniqueness deserving of special recognition. It is not required that the vineyard be the producer's own, as in cases where grapes were purchased from an independent grower who gave permission to state the vineyard's name on the label. With a successful wine, it's a winning situation for everyone—vineyard owner, wine producer, and consumer.

Napa Valley's Heitz Cellars was the first California vineyard-designated commercial wine to reach notable success. In 1966, the Heitz Martha's Vineyard Cabernet Sauvignon (not a reference to the popular Massachusetts summer destination) was that era's version of thinking outside the box. Today, it's easy to find wineries making single-vineyard wines. California's J. Lohr Winery & Vineyards, Wente Vineyards, and Dry Creek Vineyard are three brands with numerous wine selections featuring single vineyard designations.

Here's something to keep in mind: when comparing wine labels that appear identical, but are priced differently, look closely for a vineyard designation. Sometimes it's easy to miss that subtle distinction, but this detail is important because a single-vineyard wine is often more expensive. Usually, it's worth spending a little extra because a special vineyard creates a wine of distinction.

There is a unique word for distinctiveness derived from the accumulation of one-of-a-kind geographic, geologic, and climatic conditions of a single location. That word is *terroir*...

9. What is terroir?

Terroir (pronounced tear-wah) is the term for the aggregation of all factors in nature responsible for the character, style, and nuance in wine made from a specific site or region. Terroir is distinctiveness of location.

Influences of terroir include soil composition, morning or afternoon fog, day-to-night temperature swings, annual and growing-season rain, length of growing season, direction of the sun in relation to the orientation of vine rows, vineyard elevation—you get the idea: it's the totality of a site's environment, sometimes referred to as a "sense of place."

Although of French origin, terroir philosophy applies anywhere: it applies to regions like Oregon's Willamette Valley or California's Santa Maria Valley, both places where the pinot noir grape makes superb, world class wine; it applies to New York's Finger Lakes and Washington's Columbia Valley, two regions consistently producing amazing rieslings. The similarities of terroir within these regions—primarily a cool climate for pinot noir and a cold climate for riesling—create wines of notable character from identical grape varieties. This philosophy may be applied down to the details of vineyards with similar terroir.

Winegrowers and winemakers have learned how terroir is responsible for "personality" in a wine, evident year after year—except when the unpredictable nature of extreme weather intervenes...

10. What is the relationship between wine and weather?

Weather impacts a wine's overall quality, flavor, richness, ageability, complexity, and cost. Ideal grape-growing conditions bring bountiful harvests—more grapes than average years—and an abundance of wine on the market. Although it doesn't mean all of it will be high quality, you can expect a greater percentage of high quality wines than normal.

While climate differences account for why grape growers plant pinot noir in cool regions and zinfandel where it's warmer, annual variations in weather explain why the wine consumer might see higher wine prices one year or more choices of great wines in another. Every growing season has a different number of days of sun, rain, fog, mist, hail, frost and wind. What's more, the timing of any of these individual events between March and October could mean the difference between a perfect year for wine growing or a horrible crop of grapes. This is why a **vintage**—the year in which grapes were harvested—is stated on most wine labels.

Poor growing-season weather, such as severe frost or hail, can destroy or spoil crops, bringing increased prices or fewer high-quality wines, or both, from that vintage. However, it is possible to find great wines from not-so-great vintages, and vice versa. It's also possible, though rare, that a single year can produce both high volume and high quality, such as the 2012 vintage in much of California. Devoid of damaging heat spikes or frost, it was a year with a near-perfect combination of temperature, rain, and sunshine.

With the help of **vintage charts**, the growing seasons of major regions around the world can be compared. If you buy wine at specialty shops, vintage charts are normally available for reference. California's consistently good weather makes year-to-year vintage variations less significant than appellations in, say, New York State, where excessive rains one summer could ruin a vintage; or France, where irrigating vineyards during dry periods is not permitted. (That's life in a controlled appellation of origin.) Successful wines in some parts of the wine-making world depend heavily on favorable weather, so the vintage year on a label carries more meaning.

A good vintage has warm days, cool nights, and a long mild summer. A consistently cool summer ripens grapes too slowly, creating an imbalance of high acidity with low sugar, increasing tartness in that year's wines. At the other extreme, if weather conditions bring an avalanche of extremely hot days, sugar levels skyrocket and acidity virtually disappears, producing flat and heavy wines. Rain during, or nearing harvest can also upset the balance. For some delicate, thin-skinned varieties like pinot noir, excess moisture dilutes juice inside grapes and thins out wine. It may even form rot on grape clusters, reducing the amount of quality wine produced from the affected crop.

Therefore, the risk of rain spoiling the rhubarb, so to speak, increases the longer the growing season drags out...

11. What is hang time?

Knowing when to pick grapes requires a combination of timing, measurement, tasting, and gut instinct. Stretching out the length of time grapes hang on the vine requires deft skill at managing a balancing act of unpredictable weather along with almost daily changes in sugar, acid, color, and flavor of the grapes.

You might think hang time refers to how long you stick around a tasting room bar and sample the entire list of wines. Serious wine country travelers take pride in their hang time.

In the business of grape growing, however, getting more hang time means waiting longer for grapes to reach maturity and optimal ripeness; in other words, stretching out the growing season. Physiological grape maturity is determined simply by tasting grapes and observing the color of their seeds. Ripeness is determined by testing grapes for sugar and acid content. If maturity lags behind ripeness, grapes might need to hang on the vine longer than usual. But, like the hours spent inside a tasting room, adding hang time is not without risk.

The balancing act begins in August, when sugar levels from grape samples start getting regularly measured in "degrees" on a scale called **Brix**, and acidity is measured on the pH scale. Testing gives growers and winemakers an indication of ripeness and a rough idea how close they are to harvest. However, as warm daytime temperatures increase sugar development, acid levels drop. Waiting days, or weeks, to reach higher sugar levels with potential for greater flavor and alcohol in the wine also means gradually losing acidity, a vital component giving wine freshness and lively fruitiness. A wine with insufficient acidity is doomed to be flat and dull.

Grapes are typically picked at Brix readings between 22 and 28 degrees, depending on grape variety and desires of the winemaker, many of whom define hang time as the time grapes remain on the vine after they reach ripeness of 24 degrees Brix. (By the way, a final Brix reading multiplied by a "standard" conversion factor of 0.55 estimates final wine alcohol content. Thus, grapes picked at 24 degrees Brix make wine with around 13.2% alcohol.)

Wine regions with naturally long growing seasons, like California's Monterey County, benefit from longer hang time without much risk. They have consistently warm days with few heat spikes, and cool afternoons and evenings. Measured by their early budding and late ripening dates, their entire growing season may span up to a month longer than most other California appellations.

Stretching out the growing season allows grapes to develop more intense flavor, color, and complexity—all characteristics of great wines. These qualities are especially easy to appreciate while stretching your own hang time in a favorite tasting room.

12. What can be learned from a visit to a winery?

A visit to a winery not only is a fun way to get to know wine, it puts a face on a name, too. Use the opportunity to dig deep with questions about the brand's wines and maybe even meet the winemaker or owner.

Tasting rooms are always welcoming and usually your first stop on a winery visit. Their physical layouts can be as diverse as the wines themselves: from a large, lavish estate structure (Napa's Niebaum-Coppola Estate) to a small, simple garage (Sonoma's Kaz Winery). Regardless of the presentation, tasting rooms offer opportunities to discover and learn from people knowledgeable about each producer's wines. If you are unsure of what to ask as you sample their wines, here are a few questions to get the conversation going:

- "Is this wine filtered or unfiltered?"
- "Does the winery source grapes from outside its own property or are all grapes from the winery's property?"
- "How many cases of wine are produced each year?"
- "Do you offer any un-oaked wines?"
- "Before this wine was released, how long was it aged in barrel? How long in bottle?"
- "Which bottling do you consider your flagship wine"

It's interesting to learn the history of a winery and how its owner got involved in the wine business. It's surprising how many proprietors began their professional careers in areas completely outside the wine industry. In almost every case, a deep passion for wine motivated them to make the transition. Some examples:

- B. R. Cohn Winery in California's Sonoma Valley was started by the original (and current) manager of the rock band, The Doobie Brothers.
- Napa Valley's Groth Winery was founded by one of the creators of Atari video games.
- Doubleback, from Washington State, is the realization of a long-time dream of former NFL quarterback, Drew Bledsoe.

A vineyard in the peak of growing season—June through August—is picturesque, with clusters of purple or golden grapes under a bright green canopy of leaves. Even better is a winery experience during harvest, when tons of just-picked grapes head to the production facility or are already in the process of fermentation. You can sense the fragrance of freshly picked fruit mixed with notes of optimism for a new vintage.

If you are looking for a hands-on, one-day harvest adventure, check out Wine Boot Camp by Affairs of the Vine. Besides having a fun day, you get the opportunity to participate in a few vineyard and winery operations, learn wine tasting, pair wine with food, and meet winemakers, winery owners, and fellow wine enthusiasts.

If you want to experience wine country during harvest, however, book your accommodations well in advance because it's peak season for visitors...

13. What's happening at a winery during harvest?

Vineyard crews race to pick grapes in the early morning, tons upon tons of grapes arrive by the truckload at the production facility every hour, and dozens of cellar workers scramble to start the winemaking process before the next tranche of grapes are delivered. It's "all hands on deck" from August through October when everyone shares in the labor of their fruit.

Harvest season is defined by the months when ripe grapes start getting picked from vines, transported to the winery, and processed into wine. It is commonly known as **crush**. It's a stressful time for everyone involved, as tons of grapes arrive at the winery every hour, and the talent—and patience—of winemakers, assistant winemakers, lab workers, and seasonal interns are tested.

Prior to accepting the first batch of grapes, the winemaking team makes sure all of the processing equipment is thoroughly clean and in working order, all pumps and hoses rinsed and sanitized, barrels washed and dried, and yeast and chemicals at hand. The work they do and decisions they make during this busy period play an important role in how their wines will perform when released to the public—some within a year, as with most white wines, or up to four years later for some full-bodied red wines.

The day begins at dawn to pick grapes before temperatures get too hot and while fruit is still cool from overnight temperatures. Everyone involved is aware that an unexpected event could turn a year's worth of effort into disappointing results. For example, an independent grower who decided when to pick the grapes might send the winery fruit outside the winemaker's acceptable range of ripeness. It's possible the grapes could be rejected altogether and the winery will have to figure out how to make up for that loss of tonnage. If overly ripe grapes are accepted, creating a quality wine from them might require adjustments in the winemaking process—possibly the addition of acids or application of a different type of yeast than anticipated. Winemakers have to be ready for all situations.

In the coolest wine-growing regions, where grapes do not always achieve full ripeness, juice almost always needs adjusting before fermentation unless a low-alcohol wine is desired. If state wine law allows it, sugar is added—a step called chaptalization—in order to achieve acceptable alcohol content.

If you happen to be at a winery during harvest, you will see grapes trucked in from the vineyard, typically in white plastic bins, about four-feet square. Bins have the capacity to carry either one-half or one ton of grapes. Full bins of red grapes are dumped by forklift into a machine called a **destemmer-crusher,** which first separates grapes from stems and then gently crushes them to release the juices.

Sometimes a preliminary step, called **sorting**, is required to separate grapes from "**MOG,**" an abbreviation for "Material Other than Grapes;" twigs, rocks, vine leaves, and unripe and moldy grapes. The grapes are dumped onto a conveyor that leads to the destemmer-crusher. The conveyor vibrates and drops undersized grapes while workers alongside it also manually remove unwanted material.

After the destemming and crushing machine gets the winemaking process going, a maceration period follows, then fermentation, pressing, and the final step of pumping wine into tanks or oak barrels for aging.

As the day wears on, the hospitality staff is busy hosting the seasonal surge of visitors. It's an exciting time of year to be in wine country.

Know It Like the Back of Your Hand

Three keys to knowing wine imitate those for success in real estate: location, location, location. As your wine exploration continues and your taste horizons expand, you will grow increasingly curious about where the grapes for the wine in your glass were grown. The wine appellation will become as important as the grape variety itself, or even the brand.

Get in the habit of asking where a wine's grapes were grown—whether you're at a wine shop or a restaurant. When enjoying a leisurely glass of wine at home, research the wine's appellation. As you sip, read about the terroir of the appellation on its Wikipedia entry, for example, or on the producer's website.

The following appellation comparison exercises will help your understanding of wine appellations and maybe even assist in narrowing down your personal wine preferences.

- *Start large, and then go small*

Compare three different sauvignon blancs made from three different appellations: one large state appellation, one county appellation, and one small AVA. Taste and decide if the wines get more interesting and complex as the appellation gets smaller. Do they get truer to the grape varietal character with each reduction in appellation size?

Taste and compare a state appellation, Geyser Peak Winery Sauvignon Blanc "California," next to a county appellation, Dry Creek Vineyard Fumé Blanc "Sonoma County" (Fumé Blanc is another name for sauvignon blanc), next to a small American Viticultural Area, Dry Creek Vineyard Sauvignon Blanc "Dry Creek Valley."

- *A taste of two valleys*

Don't automatically associate hot weather with a valley. Many "valley" appellations include either high elevation areas with consistently cool temperatures or are influenced by nearby bodies of water. Here are two examples: Try Argyle Winery Pinot Noir "Willamette Valley" against Byron Wines Pinot Noir "Santa Maria Valley." Both appellations provide the climate in which pinot noir always thrives, but significant differences are in the soils: a combination of seabed and volcanic deposits in the Oregon bottling versus alluvial dirt and minerals in the California wine.

- *Que syrah, syrah, syrah?*

Legs, Nose, Body!

When the wine subject is syrah, three countries of origin come to mind: the U.S., Australia, and France. Compare this grape variety made in three different geographic and social cultures. Taste Qupé Syrah Central Coast from the U.S., Torbreck Woodcutter's Shiraz Barossa Valley from Australia, and E. Guigal Crozes-Hermitage Red from France.

Evaluating A Wine

ASK YOURSELF...

Are these five supporting components in balance?

and...

Does the wine represent the true varietal character?

Does the wine deliver value?

FRUIT	SWEETNESS	ACIDITY	ALCOHOL	TANNIN
Intensity of fruit flavors	Degree of sweetness or dryness	Level of crispness from acidity	Impression of weight and heat from alcohol	Impact of texture from tannin

Chapter 3

Red wine gives me a headache.

Gathering Wine Consumer Intelligence

Long before I became knowledgeable in wine, and even before I devised my "cheapest-plus-two" system for choosing the wine from a restaurant wine list, I often passed the wine list over to someone else at the table to pick out a wine. At the same time, I was intrigued by wine because its portrayal in television, movies and novels all contributed to some elusive wine mystique. I was a wine observer—an outsider who watched wine play a role in life—not mine at the time—while "insiders" chose it, drank it, enjoyed it, almost worshiped it. My curiosity was piqued.

If such things could be measured, there is probably as much mystique in wine as there are myths, both of which are addressed in this chapter and throughout the book. Wine mystique, however, is a double-edged sword: it lures new consumers to the beverage just as readily as it intimidates the uninitiated.

While I view wine mystique as both benefit and potential curse, I believe wine myth is damaging. For example, too often people express dismay that sulfites in wine are the cause of their headaches. Or, that wines made in Europe use fewer sulfites and are therefore preferable to wines made in the U.S. This chapter addresses this myth and gives plenty of other practical information to help you make smart wine decisions.

If you are digitally prepared, smartphone apps are convenient for getting information on a particular wine before purchasing.

But for those fast, on-the-spot decisions about an unfamiliar wine, the wine label is judge, jury, and executioner. Problem is, wine is a pretty complex beverage to make a purchasing decision based only on a 4-inch by 3-inch label. If you don't know what to look for, it's a roll of the dice. Fundamental knowledge of wine label information (covered in Question 19) improves your odds of making a good wine purchase.

Even if you are certain of a style of wine—say you want a light-bodied white wine—there are still all kinds of choices to make after that: grape variety; closure type (cork or twist cap); appellation (domestic wine or imported); dryness (fully dry or hint of sweetness); organic or not; new release or aged vintage? Even if you stick with familiar brands, all of these options can cause confusion and frustration if you don't understand their implications.

Read on, and no longer struggle as a wine outsider. Cut through a network of wine mystique and unravel those image-busting wine myths.

14. Do sulfites in wine give me a headache?

Sulfites, and their preservative properties, are natural byproducts of the fermentation process. Winemakers add more sulfites than what occurs in nature to keep wine fresh longer. Red wines need fewer added sulfites than white wines because tannin in red wine already acts as a preservative.

If the sulfite level in wine—and some foods—is high, it may be enough to trigger a reaction in people with an allergy to sulfites. Although individual thresholds for a reaction vary, in 1988 the U.S. government established a limit and required a label stating "Contains Sulfites" to appear on every bottle of wine made with more than the maximum allowed amount of 10 milligrams per liter. Even though a small percentage of the U.S. population, estimated to be around one percent, might sneeze or cough from drinking wine containing sulfites exceeding the limit, about ten percent of the one percent will suffer a more serious reaction, such as shortness of breath. Headaches are not a typical reaction, even though people who get them from wine usually blame the sulfites.

In the majority of cases, the cause is something else: dehydration from not drinking enough water while consuming wine; consuming wine on an empty stomach; a wine's high alcohol content; or from histamines, another natural byproduct of winemaking, present more in red wine than white. Some people take an antihistamine in advance of drinking red wine in order to prevent or mitigate a headache, or they avoid red wine altogether by choosing only white wine.

Experimenting with different producers might uncover one that makes your favorite varietal wine with the right amount of sulfites for your system. Needless to say, the cause of any physical reaction from wine is difficult to pin down without a doctor's assistance. There are dozens of compounds in wine, any one of which could cause a sensitive person to have an allergic reaction. *If you suffer any reaction as a result of drinking wine, you should consult a doctor.*

And, ask your doctor about trying wines with low sulfite content, i.e., organic wines…

15. What is organic wine?

Organic farmers and winemakers apply time-tested, "low-tech" solutions to problems in the vineyard and the winery: vineyard weeds and pests are controlled by goats and owls instead of chemicals, while wine is preserved only with sulfites produced naturally during fermentation. Organic winemaking practices have been applied successfully for centuries, long before chemicals were available. But vineyards and wineries follow organic practices not only because they're earth-friendly, but also because they believe they help make better wine.

There are certified organic wines—the closest thing to an all-natural wine—and there are wines made with organically-grown grapes, the next best alternative. The difference is significant. Producers selling wine labeled "organic" have to be independently certified in both winemaking *and* farming practices—that is, soil management, and other ecologically-friendly methods that meet strict standards of the U.S. Department of Agriculture.

If the vineyard is farmed organically, but inside the facility wine is processed independent of organic standards, the wine is not certified organic. Thus, grapes grown organically do not necessarily make organic wine. Although the grapes may have been maintained organically—without chemicals like herbicides, fungicides and pesticides—the wine *must also not exceed* a government-established, detectable sulfite limit of 10 parts per million (10mg/liter) to be organic. A typical non-organic wine might have anywhere from 25 to 80 parts per million.

Organic wines contain fewer sulfites than non-organic wines because no sulfites are *added* beyond what are produced naturally during normal fermentation. However, the majority of wines on the market do contain added sulfites, *preventing microbial activity and preserving the flavor, color, and long-term integrity of the wine.* Although an organic wine can be as flavorful and nuanced as any non-organic wine, it is typically not wine stored for long-term aging.

If you have an allergic reaction to wine, you may want to consult with a doctor about sampling wines only made from organically grown grapes. If no relief comes from that, try a 100% *certified* organic wine, which contains a reduced amount of sulfites. These wines are commonly found in natural food grocery stores or online at Organic Wine Exchange. Remember, fewer sulfites are *added* to red wine than white wine because of red wine's trademark preservative component, tannin…

16. What is tannin?

Acting as red wine's "backbone," tannin's texture and gripping facility on the palate support and preserve its partner components of alcohol, acidity, and fruit. Whereas acidity lubricates the palate by producing saliva, tannin's drying effect can be literally mouth-puckering.

Wine dryness, which provides palate-like structure for red wine, comes from **tannin**, a natural chemical compound of grape skins, seeds, stems, and oak. It's a key component of red wine and, if uncontrolled, gives wine harshness and unappealing astringency. It can do the same to wine as it does to a cup of hot tea after it cools down—make it bitter and hard to drink.

The majority of wine tannin is extracted during juice maceration and fermentation. Naturally, red wine, by virtue of its longer contact time with grape skins, has significantly more tannin, that is, dryness, than white wine. A secondary source of tannin comes from the oak barrels in which wine is aged. Wood tannin contributed by barrels varies, depending on the type of oak and toasting temperature.

Tannin also acts as a wine stabilizer, helping it age longer by protecting aroma and flavor. It enables long-term aging in bottle, a reason why you don't find as many old white wines as red. Typically, a cabernet sauvignon will show significantly more of its dry, firm tannin at two to three years old than it will after it has aged in the bottle for say, 10 years or longer. In extreme cases, a newly released cabernet can exhibit so much tannin, it becomes hard to taste any fruit at all. As wine ages, however, tannin develops a softer, silk-like texture, lessened by time but not so much as to lose its capacity to preserve the wine's delicate fruit component.

A red wine is at its peak for consumption when it has reached an age with perfect balance in tannin structure and fruit expression. Largely unpredictable to pinpoint, fine wines are known to take years, sometimes decades, to acquire that magical balance.

17. Why do some dry wines taste sweet?

Some wines are meant to taste sweet and leave no doubt with the taster. But some "dry" wines seem sweet because either the alcohol or fruit level is elevated relative to other components, causing an imbalance in the wine.

A common new-wine-drinker experience happens when you taste a dry wine and declare, "It tastes sweet!" Although it's possible for a dry wine to have a tiny amount of **residual sugar** leftover after fermentation, in most cases it is too small to be detectable on the palate. In these cases, wines give *an impression of sweetness*, but they are not sweet wines.

It's easy to be misled. Even when a wine contains zero residual sugar, an impression of sweetness might come from an oversupply of alcohol or fruit, or an insufficient level of acidity. Either high alcohol creates a sense of sweetness, or a big, bold, "fruit-bomb" wine explodes with flavor from the moment it hits your tongue and makes you think it's a sweet wine.

Just about every "dry" wine contains a tiny dose of undetectable, unfermented sugar—too small for the producer to even mention. This can work in a positive way, determined by your overall impression of the wine. It might contribute just enough to the wine to balance acidity and tannin, and allow you to focus on the wine's seamless, delicious flavor.

Wines with less than 2 grams per liter of residual sugar (sometimes stated in percentage as 0.2%) are categorized as completely dry, as the threshold for detecting sweetness starts for most people at around 4 grams per liter. But even at 4 grams per liter, sweetness still may not be noticeable because acidity balances it, making the wine taste relatively dry.

To get some perspective on residual sugar, here are examples of some popular wines with varying degrees of sweetness:

- The popular Rex Goliath Merlot, a dry wine, contains 4 grams per liter of residual sugar.
- Sweet, low-alcohol moscato, such as made by Barefoot, has residual sugar around 64 grams per liter, while some other moscatos are as high as 120 grams per liter. You are not reducing calorie consumption by choosing a low-alcohol wine with significant residual sugar.
- The classic French wine, Sauternes, viscous and elegantly sweet, has about 150 grams per liter.
- Although rare today, the world's original great sweet wine, Hungarian Tokaji Essencia (also spelled Tokay) has residual sugar content between 400 and 500 grams per liter, and sometimes higher than 800 grams!

If you read a residual sugar amount on a wine label, don't automatically think the wine will taste too sweet. Counteracting components like acidity can make residual sugar an imperceptible, but significant contributor to the wine's pleasing impression on the palate. It's all about balance.

One component perhaps more important than residual sugar, tannin, fruitiness or acidity, is alcohol. In the right amount, it is what makes fine wine...fine.

18. What is a "hot" wine?

Of all the compounds in wine, alcohol has perhaps the biggest impact on the palate, not to mention the head. As important as fruitiness, tannin, and acidity, alcohol adds weight and volume to wine. But at heightened levels alcohol may produce a hot, burning impression on the lips or inside the mouth, sensations jarring to the unsuspecting wine drinker.

Although many producers might start with high-Brix (high sugar) grapes—thus, high-alcohol potential—they believe a wine doesn't necessarily get better with more alcohol. They might take steps to remove a pre-determined amount of alcohol from wine in order to make it more balanced, food-friendly and elegant, or they could add water to the fermenting juice, although the latter approach is seldom taken. In most cases, wineries make sure grapes are picked before they develop too much sugar, reducing the potential to make a "hot" wine with over-the-top alcohol content.

Since the American wine industry's post-Prohibition rebirth in the 1960s, table wines typically had 11.5% to 12.5% alcohol. Starting around the late nineties, they quietly began climbing. It's hard to know if producers were responding to consumer demand for more robust wines or acting on a desire to imitate the higher alcohol wines winning better scores and praise. Whatever the reason, the trend seems to be abating today, making it less likely you'll come across a "hot" wine than it was years ago.

Wine labels give a sort of advance warning on how alcohol might impact your impression of the wine. It's one of several useful bits of consumer information on every wine label…

19. What should I look for on a wine label?

Unless you're looking for the name of a specific producer, shopping for a wine often means making a decision based upon what a wine label tells you. You have to look beyond the cute name or whimsical image on a label to find meaningful information worthy of influencing your wine purchasing decisions.

While a familiarity with the grape variety goes far towards predicting what's inside a bottle, you can use other bits of label information to get a rough indication of how a wine will taste.

First, let's look at what is *required on every label*:

- Brand name.
- Class or Type of wine: look for the words "Table Wine," "Dessert Wine," "Sparkling Wine," or the name of a grape variety. (A stated grape variety must comprise a minimum of 75% of the wine.) If no specific grape is indicated, the label will state "Red Wine" or "White Wine."
- Name and address of the bottling winery; if imported, the name of the importer and bottler.
- Country of origin, if an imported wine.
- Net contents, expressed in liters. A "standard" wine bottle is 750 milliliters, or 0.75 liters.
- Alcohol content, expressed in percent by volume.
- Appellation of origin of the grapes.
- A government health warning on alcohol.
- A declaration of sulfur dioxide agent ("Contains Sulfites"), if applicable. It is not required on certified organic wine.

Legs, Nose, Body!

Get accustomed to reading all the label information with special attention to the terms below:

Alcohol: As alcohol content increases, wine feels heavier on the palate, creating a more full-bodied wine style. If you are in search of a lighter, more delicate wine, either look for "**Table Wine**" on the label, meaning the alcohol content does not exceed 14%, or find wines with no more than than 13% alcohol as they tend to be more food-friendly and nuanced. If you are in search of a sweet wine, bottles labeled as "**Dessert Wine**" contains more than 14% alcohol.

Vintage: A wine's **vintage** indicates the year the grapes were harvested, *not the year the wine was bottled*. If a vintage date is stated, then 95% of the wine must be from that year and the label *must also* show a geographic origin of the grapes. For most imported wines, vintage takes on more significance than domestic wines because vineyards outside the U.S. are less likely to be irrigated and therefore subject to greater weather variables that influence wine quality from year to year.

Although red wines age longer than white wines, before choosing an old vintage red wine make sure it is an age-worthy grape variety and stored properly throughout its life. If in doubt, go with a trustworthy retailer when purchasing any wine more than five years older than the wine's current vintage on store shelves.

Bottles priced at around $25 and below are typically made for consumption when they are released to the market, whereas more expensive wines tend to do better if allowed to age longer in the bottle. It's hard to say how long—sometimes a year makes a big difference, while other wines need more time to show their best. Cellaring after buying a new wine is not a hard and fast rule, and it doesn't mean you won't enjoy a new release that costs you $50 or more. But, it's something to keep in the back of your mind if you plan to spend more on your wine choices.

Appellation of Origin: A basic appellation of origin for American wine, such as a *state* or *county*, indicates at least 75% of the grapes came from that appellation. But remember, no single state or county is an *American Viticultural Area (AVA)*, which is a *specific region* recognized for making wines of distinction. If an AVA is stated on a label it must supply a minimum 85% of the grapes. With increasing precision in the location of the grapes' appellation of origin, the characteristics of the wine become more defined. For example, a New York or Oregon appellation of origin will have fewer distinguishable characteristics than a wine from a more narrow geographic AVA designation, such as New York's Finger Lakes or Oregon's Columbia Valley.

However, keep in mind the one great advantage to a broad state appellation: it gives flexibility to the producer, allowing the winery to choose grapes from anywhere in the state—locations they likely select precisely because of superior conditions for growing certain grapes. Take, as an example, a 100% pinot noir made with the appellation "California." Assume that 50% of the grapes come from Sonoma County's Russian River AVA in northern California, and 50% from Santa Barbara County's Santa Maria Valley AVA, about 300 miles away in Central California. The appellation of origin—California—is enormous, but the grapes were grown in two of the most esteemed regions in the state for pinot noir. It's helpful when a label provides extra details like this, but it isn't required.

Beyond an appellation, a single vineyard name might be included on a label because the producer believes its unique soils and microclimate produce a special wine. Or, because the vineyard has earned a name for itself and is respected for producing wines of outstanding quality. A vineyard by itself is not an appellation of origin nor an approved American Viticultural Area.

Estate Bottled: Of less importance, but not insignificant, is the term Estate-Bottled, which can be used only if an appellation appears on the label *and* the bottling winery is located within the appellation. In addition, that wine's grapes must either have been grown on the winery's *own property*, or *controlled by the winery* if the vineyards are not owned by them. One more thing: the grapes must also have been fermented, and the wine aged and bottled, *on the winery's premises*. Whew! In other words, Estate Bottled means grapes and wine processing remained under the control of one entity from start to finish.

France has its own version of estate-bottled wines, stated on labels with the term *Mis en Bouteille au Domaine* (or *au Chateau*).

Estate-Grown: This term is not clearly and officially defined by the governing authority in charge of wine terms (the U.S. Alcohol Tax and Trade Bureau). In one case, however, it takes on more significance if the appellation is broad, such as, "California" and the grapes are owned and under the control of the producer. Take, for example, Kendall-Jackson Avant Chardonnay, which indicates the state appellation, "California." The grapes were sourced from areas scattered across the state: Monterey County, Mendocino County, Santa Barbara County and Sonoma County, each region selected for its unique contributions to the overall wine profile and quality—and all are under the ownership of Kendall-Jackson. A consumer who knows this wine's grapes were grown under one umbrella of ownership might give it an edge against another "California" appellation chardonnay made with grapes whose specifics aren't disclosed to the consumer—in most cases, purchased from sub-contracted growers. Kendall-Jackson, possibly in an effort to keep the label less cluttered, decided not to name the grape-growing regions that sourced their Avant Chardonnay, but they do list them on the downloadable tech sheet from the wine's web page.

Reserve: The term Reserve, another unofficial, unregulated term, typically identifies one of a winery's best offerings. This might mean grapes were harvested by hand instead of machine, or selected from specific vines, like only hillside vines that received the most sunlight, for example. Or, the wine was given more time in barrel for improved development. Reserve wines will usually be priced higher than a producer's non-Reserve wines.

Mandatory information on a wine label can be located on either the back or front of the bottle. With back labels, unfortunately, there's no consistency in usage. Some describe the wine's flavors and aromas, a few suggest foods for pairing, others paint a picture of the vineyard's growing conditions or give the winery's history. With blended wines, back labels that break down the compositional percentage of the various grape varieties are the most helpful.

Don't be surprised if you start seeing back labels giving complete consumer information similar to what you find on food packaging: serving portion, calories per serving, nutritional breakdown, and a list of ingredients. A few brands, like Bonny Doon Vineyard and Ridge Vineyards, are starting to do it voluntarily. If more producers follow their lead, and if consumers begin demanding the same from all producers, it might eventually become mandatory.

Finally, maybe the most important bit of consumer information is the price, although it will not give you any indication of taste or guarantee that you will enjoy it. While you expect less from bargain wines than expensive ones, low-priced wines have greater potential for giving pleasant surprises, whereas high-priced wines can lead to disappointment after building expectations.

So, you can't judge a wine by its price, and especially not its closure...

20. What's better—cork or screw cap?

It's one of the most talked about subjects among winemakers over the last decade because of a wine closure's potential to influence the quality of wine after it has been bottled. While natural cork is renewable and has proved itself for ages, it has had to answer to instances when it turns a good wine bad. On the other hand, screw caps eliminate cork's troubles and make opening bottles a breeze. But it lacks the tradition and much-loved "ceremony" of removing a cork and faces a few issues of its own.

Natural cork, the bottle closure used since commercial production of precision glass bottles, has established itself as an unofficial industry standard. An alternative to the cork closure has long been the aluminum screw cap or twist cap. It was the closure on inexpensive, low-quality wine since the sixties, resulting in a damaging association for decades. But not anymore. Since around 2000, increasingly more winemakers choose screw cap closures over natural cork for one or more of the following reasons:

- Reduced costs;
- Retained fruit freshness;
- More consistent aging;
- Reduced chance that bacteria, known as **TCA**, will impart a damp, musty smell to the wine, destroying its fruit aroma.

Another benefit of screw caps is that they allow bottles to be stored upright instead of lying on their sides. The absence of a cork closure eliminates the need to keep wine in contact with the cork, which expands to create a virtual airtight seal within the bottle.

Of all the reasons above, the problem with TCA has been the driving force behind the growing popularity and acceptance of twist caps. It is generally estimated that somewhere between 1% to 15% of all wine is tainted by natural corks containing TCA, though winemakers, cork manufacturers and wine critics have debated this number for years. In January 2013, Wine Spectator magazine's James Laube reported "3.7 percent of the 3,269 cork-sealed wines from California tasted in the Wine Spectator office in 2012 were thought to be tainted by a bad cork." If you estimate that wine aficionados at the magazine are about twice as sensitive to TCA-tainted wine than average wine consumers, it would translate to fewer than 2% *detectable by the average wine consumer*. This figure is closer to where the Cork Forest Conservation Alliance claims TCA contamination to be:

they say current testing indicates only "1% of wine is tainted by cork-TCA." Regardless of the true number, what's important is that contamination from cork is on the decline.

The smell from TCA can be too subtle for the average palate to notice, so certainly consumers have been drinking cork-tainted wines for years without knowing it. Winemakers, however, are highly sensitive to cork-taint smell and work hard to keep their products free from off-odors. That's why those winemakers who choose natural cork closures demand rigid quality control from cork suppliers. Together, they are succeeding at reducing the incidence of corked wine.

Ironically, there are issues with twist caps, as well. Because of their air-tight design, caps have on occasion been blamed for aging wines too slowly, or for a buildup of sulfides inside a bottle, which adds a subtle smell of rotten egg. Cap manufacturers responded with new technology that permits a controlled amount of oxygen into the bottle, matched to the wine style and how soon the wine will be consumed after bottling (which is difficult to know). Bottom line: there is no perfect closure.

With tens of thousands of wines entering the market every year, there is ample room for closing wines with all available options: twist caps, synthetic corks, aggregate corks (crushed natural cork pressed into a cork shape) and conventional natural corks. It has become common for twist caps to close white wines more often than reds, since they are more likely to be opened and consumed sooner. Red wines are more age-worthy and corks are proven to enhance wine-aging by allowing microscopic amounts of oxygen into the wine.

The advantages and disadvantages of various bottle closures will play out over the coming decades. Each type will find its niche. Probably alternative closures will close the more affordable wines and corks the more expensive wines. But who knows? One thing is sure: no longer is the twist cap associated with cheap, inferior wine. Perhaps more important, you shouldn't fret over purchasing wines closed with natural corks. With any closure, odds are greatly in favor of the consumer getting a flawless wine—red or white, young or old.

21. Are older wine vintages better than younger ones?

While stating wine gets better with age may be sage advice, it isn't necessarily true. There are certainly some older wines you will enjoy more than younger ones, and vice versa. But you generally pay more for ageability in a wine, and then can only guess at when it will be at its peak.

Several years ago I attended an historic wine tasting at Niebaum-Coppola Winery, hosted by film legend and winery owner, Francis Ford Coppola. At the event, he poured estate cabernet sauvignon made under the original Niebaum brand—which later became the Inglenook brand—from before the time he purchased the winery, and after. He served one wine from each of the eight decades of the wine estate's history, from the 1930s to the 2000s.

If I had scored the wines from "outstanding" down to "good," the results would not have followed a straight line starting with the oldest and ending with the youngest. In other words, the older vintages were not necessarily better than the younger ones. Although every wine was compelling and had its own personality, my favorites were scattered randomly throughout the eight decades. Despite an expectation that older wines would be better, my favorite wine was among the youngest in the group.

Studies have determined that 80% of wine is consumed *within 48 hours* of purchase. So it's not surprising that most American wines are made to be consumed young—within 1 to 2 years of the vintage—and will not improve much with long-term bottle aging. However, you can count on older red wines to have more complexity and smoothness than younger vintages—and *some* of the older wines in my Coppola tasting did.

If you were to graph the change in red and white wines as they age, it would rise gradually and reach a peak of overall performance in some future year, and then start to curve downward in subsequent years of declining performance. It is an educated guess by winemakers and wine critics as to when that peak will come for any given wine. This is why some people purchase age-worthy wines by the case, store it for long-term, and then open one bottle every few years to taste—and estimate—when that aging curve will peak.

Even though the absence of tannin in white wines eliminates a major natural preservative, it is possible for well aged white wines to provide a tasting experience just as memorable as an aged red wine. It's just harder to discover them. If you're looking for an age-worthy white wine, you may want to start your search with French wines after asking for assistance from your local wine merchant.

Know It Like the Back of Your Hand

Two key components impacting your impression of a wine are tannin and alcohol. If either one is out of balance with fruit and acidity, your opinion of the wine will likely tend toward negative. So before you can decide if everything's in balance, it's important to learn to recognize tannin and alcohol when you feel it on the palate…not your head!

One of the exercises below demonstrates how tannin texture can vary in red wines, depending on the grape variety. While tannin in both wines in the exercise have a drying effect on the palate and work in balance with other components, one is firm and rigid enough to support a bigger wine, while the other is soft and round, appropriate for a more delicate wine.

The other exercise shows how alcohol impacts the overall weight and presence of wine on the palate. Because of alcohol's effects on your ability to think and react, you need to understand how you can be deceived by a well balanced, high alcohol wine. The better the wine is crafted with complementary amounts of alcohol, acidity, tannin and fruit, the more pleasing the wine will be, possibly inviting too much to be consumed too quickly. (That's why it's good to get into the habit of checking alcohol content on the label before you taste.) If the wine feels "hot" right away, you have a built-in reminder of the alcohol content with every sip. However, if you sense an irresistable and seamless integration of all components, be conscious of your intake.

Make the following taste comparisons to get a feel—literally—for tannin and alcohol on your palate. It is not necessary to compare wines in the same price category.

- Taste pinot noir from Oregon, such as A to Z Wineworks (*a soft, low-impact tannin*) with a newly-released Napa Valley cabernet sauvignon, like from Franciscan Estate (*a drier, high-impact tannin*);
- Taste an 11 % alcohol, dry riesling from Washington, like Chateau Ste. Michelle Eroica Riesling (*a light, refreshing impression on the palate*) next to a Silverado Carneros Chardonnay with over 14% alcohol (*a full-bodied, heavier wine that feels warm on the lips and palate*).

Popular Wine Styles As They Are Known In The US And France

Americans Know It As...	In France, It's Known As...
Cabernet Sauvignon	Red Bordeaux
Merlot	Red Bordeaux
Sauvignon Blanc	White Bordeaux
Pinot Noir	Red Burgundy
Chardonnay	White Burgundy
Syrah and Grenache	Red Rhone
Viognier	White Rhone
Sparkling Wine	Champagne

Chapter 4

I'll take a glass of the house red.

Navigating A Network of Wine Grapes and Styles

In the 1960s, I grew up in a home with a one-gallon jug of red wine always in the refrigerator. I don't remember ever opening it and not seeing that jug of wine. I think it came with the refrigerator.

As I recall, my parents typically drank wine with dinner. But on holidays there was no question about whether that jug would make its appearance. On these special days, it was ceremoniously taken from its chilled quarters and placed *on the floor* next to my father's place at the table. Our "house red" was Gallo Hearty Burgundy, still popular today.

Unknown to my parents at the time, their Hearty Burgundy had *nothing to do with Burgundy, France, nor was it made from pinot noir grapes—the two components that define a red Burgundy wine!* (I don't think they cared, either.) To be fair, the wine might have contained a small percentage of pinot noir, as in Gallo's Hearty Burgundy today, but it bore no resemblance to the aroma, flavor, or delicacy of a true red Burgundy wine.

Also in the refrigerator was a jug of a white wine called Chablis, another misnomer because Chablis is also a region of France (a sub-appellation within Burgundy) and it is always made with chardonnay. Needless to say, there was no mention of the chardonnay grape anywhere on the label. (I appreciate now my father's ingenuity fitting *two* one-gallon jugs of wine in the same refrigerator.)

During the decades when the American wine industry rebuilt itself after Prohibition, it was common practice for producers to describe the style of their wines using the names of better known wines from around the world—even though the only similarity between the wine made in the U.S. and the original wine (whether from France, Italy, or Germany) was the color! If it was red, it was labeled Burgundy, Bordeaux, or Chianti. If it was a white wine, it was called Chablis! Like my parents, most American consumers were not fussy about what grapes made the wine. The more knowledgeable wine drinker, however, knew these wines could not possibly be what the labels claimed.

By the seventies, California producers started using the name of the grape variety to identify the wine. This was a risky step because most consumers didn't know what "pinot noir" meant, but they knew what to expect when "Burgundy" was on the label. (They knew the wine was red!) As grape variety identification of wine grew popular, a more sophisticated American wine consumer grew with it.

Today, grape variety identification on American wines has become an unofficial industry standard. Alternately, a wine is given a unique name entirely, as often done when made from a combination of several grapes, none of which is at least 75% of the total. If no grape varieties are identified on the label, the wine can be called anything—even Hearty Burgundy!

Wines from France, like many European wines, are traditionally identified only by wine region. However, more exports to the U.S. now state the grape variety on the label in an effort to appeal to the American wine consumer, unfamiliar with French wine regions. Wines from Italy can be the most confusing. (If you've ever been to Italy, you are not surprised at this.) They identify some wines by region, others by grape variety, and some with both.

If you don't care about anything more than the color of your wine, it is perfectly okay to ask for a glass of house red at a restaurant. You are taking chances, though, because the quality of your wine experience depends on the quality of the wines served at that establishment. Restaurants that don't sell a lot of wine have the most limited wine lists—which could be why they do not sell much wine. And their "house red" (or white) will likely come from the lowest price tier of that list, further reducing your chances of getting a decent wine.

So, with a little knowledge of wine styles and grape varieties, there is no reason to order by color alone. When you allow the restaurant to choose the wine, you may end up with a glass poured from a refrigerated jug wine!

22. Why don't European wine labels state the name of the grape?

When over centuries, an appellation consistently makes a wine style of singular, world-class quality, the region's name becomes synonymous with that wine style. The long history of European winemaking has enabled this association. Consumers around the world need no more detail about a wine other than an appellation in order to know what to expect.

Until U.S. appellations achieve similar status, the majority of American wine consumers need and expect to see the name of a grape variety on a label—and to rely on a brand's reputation—to anticipate the style of wine in the bottle.

It took over a thousand years for European grape growers and wine producers to learn which variety performs best in each grape-growing region. Once they got it down, these appellations of origin pumped out the best wines in the world. As one extraordinary wine after another became associated with its region of origin, wine lovers everywhere grew accustomed to identifying one of these great wines simply by the name of its appellation: "Bordeaux", "Burgundy", "Chablis", "Beaujolais."

The region name was prominent on the bottle or barrel along with the producer's name. The grape or grapes that made it famous, however, remained somewhat anonymous. Referred to as "noble" grapes, they included cabernet sauvignon and merlot in the making of Bordeaux's famous blended wines; pinot noir for fine red Burgundy wine; chardonnay in white Burgundy and its sub-region's steely white wine, Chablis; and gamay for making fresh and fruity wines from Beaujolais, another sub-region of Burgundy.

Furthermore, the brand names producing these extraordinary wines also became associated with these celebrated appellations.

For example, French wine estates in Bordeaux such as Chateau Latour, or Chateau Lafite-Rothschild were automatically linked to their sub-appellation, Médoc, renowned for its refined, sumptuous, medium-to-full-bodied red wine. Although the wines were made from the five classic Bordeaux grape varieties familiar to us today, that didn't matter as much as their Bordeaux (specifically, Médoc) pedigree.

Many of the wine styles of Europe that we recognize today became synonymous with their regions a couple of hundred years ago. Here are the most popular styles with the corresponding grapes that made their wines great—and world famous:

Bordeaux Wine: Reds are primarily made with **cabernet sauvignon** or **merlot**; a few are single-varietal wines, but most wines are blends of both grapes. Other varieties of the region, sometimes referred to as blending grapes, include **cabernet franc**, **malbec** and **petit verdot**. Many producers blend all five varieties into one wine. Bordeaux white wines are made from the **sauvignon blanc** or **sémillon** grape, as well as blended versions of these two grapes..

Burgundy Wine: Pinot noir is the only grape in this region's famous sensuous red wine, sourced from its most legendary sub-region, Côte d'Or. **Chardonnay** is the grape that makes its soft, medium-to-full-bodied white wines.

Chablis Wine: Made in a northern sub-appellation of Burgundy, **chardonnay** is grown in mineral rich soil and a climate cooler than the rest of Burgundy, making a steely, lean version of the classic white grape.

Beaujolais Wine: From another sub-appellation of Burgundy, this easy drinking, fruity red wine is made with a grape called **gamay**. Serve slightly chilled to bring out its vibrant fruit flavor.

Rhone Wine: Red wines are made primarily with the **syrah** or **grenache** grape, including blends of these and other red and white grapes. Most white wines from the Rhone Valley use

viognier, **roussanne**, and **marsanne** grapes, either alone or in blends.

Châteauneuf-du-Pape Wine: A complex red Rhone wine made from up to 13 different grapes including **grenache**, **syrah**, **mourvedre**, **cinsault**, **counoise**, and **viognier**.

Chianti Wine: Made in a sub-appellation of Italy's Tuscany region, this wine is primarily made with the **sangiovese** grape. Italy takes both approaches to wine identification. Some popular wines, like Chianti, Valpolicella and Barolo are geographic names, while wines labeled as prosecco (a sparkling wine), barbera, and pinot grigio, are wines named after grapes. Brunello di Montalcino is an example that uses both a grape name *and* place of origin: Brunello is the original name for sangiovese and Montalcino is a town within Tuscany.

The United States, a relative latecomer in the long history of wine, takes a different approach to wine identification than the Europeans. If you want to sell to wine consumers in America, the opposite applies: if you don't associate a grape variety with the wine, you risk confusing the buyer. A convincing story by one American wine retailer, Dave Clark of San Diego's Wine Connection, says it best:

"A number of years ago, I worked for a large discount-oriented wine store that often bought entire lots of interesting wines and sold them at steep discounts. Once, we purchased the entire inventory of a regional distributor and found ourselves with a huge amount of very fine Chablis wines from a recent and excellent vintage. We put out floor stacks of these wonderful white Burgundies at $9.99 a bottle and they just sat there!

Hundreds of customers simply walked past some of the best deals they were ever likely to see with little more than a quick glance. As I was sitting at home with friends enjoying a fantastic bottle of one of these, it hit me. They didn't know what a Chablis was! They think this is some low-grade jug wine because of the Chablis name.

The next day I re-labeled the floor displays to read prominently "100% Chardonnay from Burgundy France" and the wines took off! We made a lot of friends for the store with that deal and introduced a number of customers to the pleasures of fine French wine."

Since the late nineties, in an effort to increase sales to American consumers, a growing number of French wines have been labeled with a grape variety, but their custom of identifying wine by region still dominates.

Another trademark of French wine identification is their official classification, or ranking, of *individual wine estates* according to quality. The higher the wine quality, the higher the classification, or *cru* (pronounced "crew"), which translates to "growth." The desire to rank by quality originally came from 18th century wine merchants and brokers in Bordeaux's Médoc region. They figured, since their best wines fetched the highest prices among the best wines in the world, a ranking by quality was essentially a ranking by price, with some consideration also given to an estate's terroir. In their eyes, a classification of chateaus helped consumers make smarter wine purchases. Thus, a higher "growth" level (cru) was a more prestigious "seal of approval" for the chateau than a lower level cru. In 1855, the first "official" list of classifications was established. It ranked 61 estates into five levels of growth classes—and it has been virtually unchanged ever since.

As you might suspect, France's Burgundy appellation created its own system of quality classification, making the examination of all of France's various appellation and sub-appellation classifications terribly complex and sometimes confusing—especially because they don't all use the same terms for class levels. Each region's system originated long ago as a subjective ranking of wine quality and is still recognized and applied to their wines today.

A thumbnail summary follows:

- Médoc's highest-level wines are called First Growth, or *Premier Cru*. Only five estates qualify as First Growth out of 61 across all class levels stepping down from First to Fifth Growth.
- Non-classified wines of the Médoc are categorized into three incrementally higher quality levels: from basic *Crus Bourgeois*, to *Crus Grands Bourgeois*, to *Crus Grands Bourgeois Exceptionnel*.
- Other sub-appellations of Bordeaux, namely Sauternes-Barsac, Graves, and Saint-Emilion, each have their own versions of classification systems.
- Burgundy's highest quality rank is *Grands Cru*, stepping down from there to *Premiers Cru*, down again to village-named wines, and then less esteemed, regional-named wines.

In the United States, there are no wine quality classification systems, nor cabernet sauvignons recognized around the world simply as "Napa Valley Red." But some American appellations are slowly establishing themselves as specialists in certain grapes after decades of trial and error with different grape varieties. These AVAs are becoming associated with a single grape because of exceptional wines being consistently produced within their borders. Examples are:

- Pinot noir from Oregon's Willamette Valley and California's Russian River Valley, Santa Barbara County, and Santa Lucia Mountains;
- Cabernet sauvignon from California's Napa Valley and Washington's Columbia Valley;
- Riesling from Washington and New York's Finger Lakes;
- Chardonnay from California's Carneros, Santa Maria Valley, and Sonoma Coast;

- Syrah, grenache, and zinfandel from California's Paso Robles region.

Lastly, a more generalized, continental breakdown of wine styles can be made: the so-called, **New World** wine producing countries of the U.S., Australia, New Zealand, Chile, Argentina, and South Africa tend to make red wines with more intense, full-body, high-alcohol style than the **Old World** wine countries of France, Italy, Germany and Spain. Historically, the latter group has made more nuanced, moderate-alcohol wines. However, the power and depth of Italian Barolo and French Hermitage are two examples, among others, that break the delicate, European style convention. And many New World producers, particularly American brands, have reversed a trend toward bigger wines by offering many wines made with moderate alcohol, balance, and finesse.

23. How are claret, Meritage, and Bordeaux wines different from each other?

Although American Meritage is stylistically different from French Bordeaux—also known as claret—they are both blends made from the classic red grapes of Bordeaux.

Claret (pronounced clair-ette), is a common British term for a classic French red Bordeaux blend. Centuries ago, the term was spelled clairet and applied to a red Bordeaux more lightly colored than today's darker, fuller style.

Meritage (rhymes with heritage) is a protected name applying only to an American wine blend of any combination of red Bordeaux grapes—a sort of American version of claret or red Bordeaux. Another Meritage qualification: no single grape variety can make up more than 90% of the blend. Meritage wines are frequently given unique names, also known as "fanciful" names, like Symmetry by Rodney Strong or Stature by Kendall-Jackson.

Whether a wine is claret, Meritage, or Bordeaux, each is characterized by a medium-to-full body mouthfeel and richness featuring notes of blackcurrant, plum, cedar, and tobacco. Most often, this style of wine pairs seamlessly with meat dishes.

To learn more about Meritage wines, visit Meritage Alliance: meritagealliance.com

24. Are syrah and petite sirah the same wines?

Although they differ in flavor and style—one spicy, the other jammy— there is a genetic connection between the two. It has been established through DNA research that syrah and a grape called peloursin are the biological parents of petite sirah.

Petite sirah, also known as durif, is usually used as a blending grape for adding color, tannin, and intensity of fruit flavor. It is not uncommon to find this grape as a single varietal wine, though fewer than ten percent of U.S. producers make petite sirah. The grape can create a delicious and interesting wine with dense, inky quality, blackberry flavor, and a long smoky finish. In fact, there isn't anything petite about it, except for its small berry diameter and cluster size. If you like big, bold, red wine, you will like petite sirah. Check out PS, I Love You, an organization of petite sirah producers. They conduct tasting events open to the public—a fun way to experience this special varietal.

Syrah, known in Australia as **shiraz**, is more frequently made as a single-varietal wine. The color is less intense than petite sirah, though not without strong and mouthwatering flavor. Naturally peppery, syrah is a popular choice to serve with beef stews and flavorful dishes made with game. Its geographic home has long been associated with the north-south-running Rhone Valley, a controlled wine appellation in the Southeast section of France. Famous syrah-based wines from the Rhone Valley are Côte Rôtie and Hermitage, representing syrah's full potential as a forward, spicy wine of deep ruby color.

25. Is there an easy way to navigate a wine list?

The more extensive the wine list the more likely you'll find values at the lower price levels. Conversely, limited, economically-minded list usually offers its best values in the high price tier. Also, once you get familiar with the different types of lists, it's clear sailing to making a great choice for the occasion.

Wine lists can be a pet peeve for wine lovers who dine out often. For many, deciding on a restaurant depends more on who has the best choices on the wine list, rather than the menu. Further, typical markups for wine range from two to two-and-a-half times retail price.

Finding a wine that fits your needs for dinner is easy when you have a foundation of wine knowledge, including familiarity with grape varieties and awareness of the three most common list formats, described below. You will probably grow to prefer one format over another, but if you are fortunate to have a digital tablet wine list handed to you, like the ones provided throughout the network of Flemings Steakhouses, for example, you can sort wines any way you please.

A **progressive wine list** categorizes the restaurant's wines *according to style* and arranges them starting with the lightest, most delicate white wines, typically sparkling wines, and finishing with full-bodied, intense red wines like zinfandels, syrahs, petite sirahs and blends of these grapes. This is the easiest type of wine list to navigate if you are still early in your journey to wine savvy. You simply choose a wine either based on your mood, personal preference, or style that best matches the intensity of flavor of the food that will pair with the wine.

A **geographic wine list** breaks down wines *by country or wine growing region*. Most geographic wine lists are geographic-progressive, categorizing wines first by country and appellation, and then further sorting wines progressively, from light-body to full-body. It helps to be familiar with the styles of wine and the popular grapes from each region to be able to make an optimal choice of wine for your meal.

A **varietal wine list** breaks down wines *by grape variety*, listing them in progressive order of style, from light white wine to heavy red wine. This is popular among restaurants with wine lists entirely comprised of American-made wines. If imported wines are offered, a separate grouping on the list displays those wines. To best navigate a varietal wine list, become familiar with the true varietal character of each grape so you know what to expect in terms of fruit flavor and mouthfeel. It also helps if you know a little about wine appellations that are widely acknowledged to produce great wines of a certain style.

26. What is a Rhone-style wine?

Rhone-style wines rally around two primary grapes: bold, dark, and spicy syrah and the peppery, raspberry-tinged grenache grape. Either as single-varietal wines or as blends, Rhone wines are robust, full-bodied, and mouthwatering.

Twelve out of France's 22 Rhone Valley grapes are grown in the United States, where most producers blend two or more into Rhone-style wines. The most popular reds combine syrah, grenache, and mourvedre grapes, while viognier, marsanne and roussanne are white grapes most frequently made either as single-varietal white wines or as blends.

Syrah, probably the most recognized Rhone grape, has grown in popularity among American wine drinkers since the nineties. Not even in the list of top ten grapes planted in California then, today syrah is a serious challenger to cabernet and merlot in popularity among red wine drinkers. It has earned its place among the leaders for its depth of character, dense, dark fruit layers that explode with plum and blackberry, and enticing notes of exotic spice and cocoa. It has a tannic backbone to complement its bold fruit, but normally is not as rigid as cabernet sauvignon or petite sirah. Syrah is often paired with game dishes or beef prepared with rich or spicy gravy.

Grenache and mourvedre, less popular than syrah, but elegant grapes still, are often blended with syrah to add finesse. Grenache leans to lighter berry characteristics of strawberry and raspberry, whereas mourvedre tends to have more blackberry flavor and angular mouthfeel. Some American blends are referred to simply as **GSM**: Grenache-Syrah-Mourvedre, because these three stars of the Rhone have become so successful working together.

The most recognized regional wine name from the Rhone Valley is Châteauneuf-du-Pape, a small sub-region of the Valley. It can range in style from a layered wine with understated fruit to a more robust and muscular mode that resembles the bold, California GSM style.

Finally, viognier (pronounced vee-ohn-yay) is a white grape of the Rhone that makes a full-bodied, aromatic wine with smooth texture, flavors reminiscent of melon, and aromas of fresh flowers. Interestingly, viognier, along with roussanne and marsanne, is frequently blended with red grapes to boost the aroma of a Rhone-style red wine. As single-varietal wines, roussanne and marsanne make full-bodied white wines with hints of honey and herbs.

For more information about Rhone-style wines, check out these two organizations:

Rhone Rangers: rhonerangers.org

Hospice du Rhone: hospicedurhone.org

27. What is Beaujolais Nouveau?

Only one commercial red wine is consumed within weeks of its grapes coming off the vines and made specifically for short term aging—measured in weeks, not years. It is Beaujolais Nouveau, from Beaujolais, France. The best in this bright, fruity red wine comes out when served slightly chilled.

From grapes harvested in September, the juice for Beaujolais Nouveau wine is fermented quickly and bottled immediately for quick release to the world, traditionally on the third Thursday of November.

Made from grapes grown in the Beaujolais sub-region of Burgundy, Beaujolais Nouveau is always a red wine made from a grape called gamay, a variety used by fewer than one percent of all producers in the U.S. Due to a closed-tank fermentation process called **carbonic maceration**, it is light in color, low in alcohol, and mild in tannin. It is a bright, fruity wine—a good starter wine for life-long soft drink consumers.

Beaujolais Nouveau is created exclusively for the purpose of drinking in its infancy and should not be put away for long-term aging. Nearly all of its production is sold and consumed between Thanksgiving and New Year's Day. If you happen to see bottles of Beaujolais Nouveau on store shelves by Easter, proceed with caution—it is past its prime consuming period.

Beaujolais Nouveau is also a very affordable wine. It is often sold at around $10 a bottle, rarely more than $20 a bottle. Because it is a simple and refreshing wine, it pairs well with a variety of foods, except for hearty, full-flavored dishes.

28. What are Late Harvest wines? Port, Sherry, and Madeira wines?

Noticeable residual sugar is the hallmark of any dessert wine. While some get their sweetness from grapes picked late in the season when more sugar has accumulated, others allow a grape fungus to dry up the grapes and amass a soaring sugar-to-juice ratio. Sweetness in Port, Sherry, and Madeira is achieved by halting fermentation early (retaining residual sugar) by the addition of high-alcohol grape spirit (brandy) to must.

Picking grapes late in the growing season to increase sugar content creates a style called **Late Harvest**, a sweet wine commonly made from riesling, zinfandel, or moscato, among other grape varieties. Some Late Harvest styles are created by allowing grapes—usually sauvignon blanc or sémillon—to become dried and shriveled like raisins from rot or fungus called **Botrytis,** leaving a high concentration of sugar inside the grapes. The most famous example of botrytized wine is **Sauternes**, the legendary and highly valued French dessert wine.

Another approach to making sweet wine is to introduce a high-alcohol, grape-based spirit or brandy to the fermentation of juice while residual sugar exists in the must. This produces a sweet wine with anywhere from 15% to 22% alcohol, depending on the point at which the spirit is added. This is how **Port**, **Sherry**, and **Madeira** wines are made. Each has its own style and traditional methods of manufacture.

Port

Port wine, named after *Porto*, a city in Portugal where the wine originated, is made from as many as 48 different grape varieties. Blending the must with clear, high-alcohol brandy stops the fermentation process halfway through, leaving significant sugar in the wine. Two popular Port wines, **Ruby Port** and **Tawny Port,** are made affordable by blending wines from different years—thus, a specific single vintage year does not appear on the label. Ruby Port, aged for four years before being marketed, is less expensive than Tawny Port, which is aged longer, usually in increments of 10, 20, 30, or 40 years. Tawnys stating the aging term period on the label are more expensive—and of superior quality—than Tawnys that do not. As their names imply, Ruby Port is ruby red and Tawny Port has a brownish hue.

In spring, immediately following rare years of exceptionally good weather, a Port producer may declare the previous vintage deserving of a **Vintage Port** moniker. Only about three times a decade are growing conditions good enough to earn this distinction. When they are, a producer will boast this rare event by stating the vintage year of harvest on the bottle. Once Vintage

Port is bottled, it will typically get 10 years or more of bottle aging before marketed. Only about 1% to 3% of all Port wines available today are Vintage Ports.

Another popular style is **Late-Bottled Vintage** Port (LBV). The style is between that of a blended-year Port (Ruby or Tawny), and a Vintage Port. It is made from a single vintage, but from grapes grown in better-than-average years, *not the very best years.* LBV Port is aged in oak barrels four to six years.

Madeira

Madeira wine, named after an island off the Portuguese coast, is made by stopping fermentation early with a dose of high-alcohol brandy, leaving significant sugar in the wine and bumping up the alcohol. Sometimes the addition of brandy comes after fermentation is completed, resulting in a less sweet wine.

Madeira manufacture is unique, the result of a long-term aging process wherein the wine is exposed to heat, then cooling to build a very durable, age-worthy wine. This pre-oxidizing "cooking" process helps the finished wine survive poor storage conditions that would normally spoil other wines.

Two Madeira styles are **Sercial** and **Verdelho**, examples where brandy is added late to create a drier wine. **Bual** and **Malmsey** are wines made with early dosing of brandy, leaving more sugar in the wine to create a fuller, sweeter style.

Sherry

Sherry, a Spanish wine, is a non-vintage wine made by a complex system of blending younger Sherry with older Sherry across multiple years. The addition of grape brandy after the original wine has completed fermentation fortifies Sherry usually to 15% to 17% alcohol, depending on the specific style desired.

The light, dry style is **Fino** Sherry, which breaks down further into **Manzanilla**, **Amontillado**, and **Pale Cream** Sherry, differentiated by variations in color and flavor. Manzanilla has a delicate salty character; Amontillado is deep amber with a nuttier taste, and Pale Cream Sherry light in color and body. Because of their delicate nature, Fino and Manzanilla Sherry are best served from a newly opened bottle, as they will not keep their fresh style more than a few months thereafter.

The darker, heavier style is **Oloroso** Sherry—higher in alcohol than Fino, and made either sweet or dry. The sweetest are **Cream** Sherry and the rare **Pedro Ximénez** Sherry.

29. What is the difference between Champagne and sparkling wine?

All Champagne is sparkling wine, but not all sparkling wine is Champagne. Authentic Champagne is made in the region in France named Champagne.

All wines with bubbles produced naturally by carbon dioxide gas fall under the broad category of sparkling wine. However, genuine Champagne specifically comes from the famous chalky soil wine region in France called Champagne and is made by a traditional, labor- and time-intensive method known as **méthode champenoise**: Champagne method. You also might see the term **méthode traditionnelle** (traditional method) on the label of méthode champenoise Champagne.

The grapes that make French Champagne's *base wine*—that is, *still wine, not sparkling*—are chardonnay, pinot noir, and pinot meunier. Sometimes a base wine is made only from one grape, such as chardonnay, as in the case of Blanc-de-Blancs Champagne, literally, white from white; or only from pinot noir, as with Blanc-de-Noir (white from black). Most Champagnes, however, are made by blending all three grapes. (Three other grapes are permitted, but rarely used: pinot blanc, petit meslier and arbane.)

Through international trademark law, wineries around the world are no longer permitted to identify a sparkling wine as Champagne if the grapes are from outside the Champagne region of France—it is a protected appellation name. Even in France, sparkling wine made outside the Champagne region must be identified as **crémant**, not Champagne.

A few American producers are grandfathered-in, and can label their sparkling wine as Champagne if they choose, while others ignore the law altogether and still print "Champagne" on the label. Most, however, use the more generic "sparkling wine." One term, "Champagne style," gets around the law. It is permitted on an American-made sparkling wine if it was made in the traditional Champagne method.

Sparkling wines around the world are identified differently, each country applying their own term. For example:

- In Spain, it is labeled **cava;**
- In Germany, it's known as **sekt;**
- In Italy, the word is **spumante** (**frizzante** if milder effervescence).

When reading a Champagne label, you might see the phrase "**Fermented in This Bottle.**" It means the **second fermentation**, which produces the bubbles, occurred *inside that bottle*. This is what defines traditional méthode champenoise, widely acknowledged to produce smaller, longer-lasting bubbles, and a superior quality of sparkling wine—albeit at a higher cost. A mild "toastiness" originates from the yeast of the second fermentation, which comes after dead yeast cells from the first fermentation have been removed and a small amount of sweetened reserve wine, called *dosage*, is added, along with yeast, to the base wine inside the bottle.

If the traditional method is not used, the label will usually indicate that either the **Charmat** (also called Tank or Bulk) method or **Transfer** method was used. These are two inexpensive and frequently used methods for making sparkling wine. The second fermentation (the one that creates the sparkle) is formed inside a large container or tank, *not inside the bottle that* *contains the sparkling wine.* Because these methods do not use a traditional, time-consuming process of manually shifting dead yeast sediment, and then removing it, one bottle at a time, (steps called riddling and disgorging), they instead send the sparkling wine in bulk through a pressurized tank for filtering, then re-bottling—*in different bottles.* Therefore, labels on these sparkling wines may indicate "Bottle-Fermented," however it will not say "Fermented in *This* Bottle."

Vintages are treated differently with Champagne wine. It is quite common for French Champagne to be labeled without indicating a specific vintage year. Thus, a **Non-Vintage** Champagne might have the letters **NV** on the label, meaning wines from two or more vintages were blended to make the base wine. The blending is done to create a consistent "house style" year after year, which is not always possible in a cool region such as Champagne. In some years grapes barely achieve ripeness, so wine saved from previous years is blended with the current year to balance out annual variations in quality. A non-vintage Champagne is priced lower than one made entirely from the best grapes grown in a single, rare year of superior weather, which is when **Vintage Champagne** is made, indicated by a specific year stated on the label. Finally, if the term **cuvée** is on the label, it denotes the wine came from the highest quality juice from the first pressing of grapes.

For more fine points of French Champagne, savor these tidbits:

- French Champagne can be sold by producers who *do not grow grapes* of their own and who, instead, purchase grapes to make Champagne. These producers are **Négociants**, and the letters **NM** (Négociant Manipulant) will be in small print on the label indicating the Champagne was made with purchased grapes.

- *If they grow their own grapes,* the product is called Grower Champagne, and the letters **RM** (Récoltant Manipulant) will appear.
- The letters **RC** (Récoltant Coopérateur) indicate the producer is a member of a cooperative that makes and sells the Champagne *under the producer's name.*
- If all the grapes of the cooperative are pooled together and *sold as a cooperative brand,* the label will indicate **CM** (Coopérative Manipulant).
- **MA** (Marque d'Acheteur) means the brand is not a grower or a producer, or a cooperative, but *an outside party.*
- **ND** (Négociant Distributeur) appears on the label when a *wine merchant* is selling the Champagne under its own name.

One last thing to remember when shopping for Champagne and sparkling wines: terminology used to describe the level of dryness can be confusing. Particularly unexpected is the use of the term "Extra-Dry," which, in the lingo of Champagne, means a small amount of sweetness is detectable—just the opposite of what you might think. Here's how Champagne terms translate:

- **Brut Nature** or **Extra Brut** has less than 6 grams per liter of sugar, sometimes stated as 0.6% residual sugar. (Extreme dryness.)
- **Brut** has up to 15 grams of sugar per liter, the most popular Champagne style. Sweetness may not be obvious because it is balanced with high acidity. ("Normal" dryness.)
- **Extra-Dry or Extra-Sec** has 12 to 20 grams per liter of sugar. (Some noticeable sweetness.)
- **Sec** has 17 to 35 grams per liter of sugar. (Medium sweetness.)
- **Demi-Sec** has 33 to 50 grams per liter. (High sweetness.)

- **Doux** has over 50 grams of sugar per liter—5% residual sugar. (Extreme sweetness.)

<u>Know It Like the Back of Your Hand</u>

Start your wine styles training the same way a lot of today's seasoned wine professionals did decades ago: with Chablis by Gallo. It's an example of an American brand using the name of a French appellation, which was not an unusual way to market wine back in the sixties. It obviously worked for Gallo, as they continue to make this popular wine in 1.5 liter and 3 liter sizes. But when you taste it next to genuine French Chablis—made in the region of France with the same name—you immediately get the difference. To be fair, the American Chablis by Gallo is sold at a ridiculously lower price than true Chablis from France. It is an example of a mass-produced, affordable, American wine. But the lesson here is not just about identification of wines. It's also about style.

Knowing different styles of wine enables you to make better choices, depending on the food you are pairing it with or your mood. After taking the Chablis taste test, try these other side-by-side comparisons that demonstrate differences in wine styles. *Do your best to get comparably priced wines in each matchup*:

- Compare a red Bordeaux from France, an Old World style—defined by *delicate mouthfeel, mild fruit, soft oak impact, and earthy nuance*—with a Meritage from California, a New World style with bold, *lush fruit and noticeable oak and power.*
- Compare *dry,* sparkling Brut Champagne with *sweet,* sparkling Sec Champagne.
- Compare a light red wine style Beaujolais Nouveau, from France (*bright fruit, light-bodied, served slightly chilled*)

Legs, Nose, Body!

with a big, bold style California zinfandel (*dark fruit, full-bodied, served room temperature*) Note: Beaujolais Nouveau is best from mid-November until the New Year. If not available, choose a Beaujolais Villages appellation.

Suggested Wines To Pair With Popular Foods

	Red Wines	White Wines & Rosé
MEATS		
Beef	pinot noir, cabernet sauvignon, merlot, syrah	
Pork & Veal	pinot noir	chardonnay
Lamb	pinot noir, cabernet sauvignon, merlot	
Stews	cabernet sauvignon, merlot, syrah, zinfandel	
Ham	pinot noir, zinfandel	sauvignon blanc
Game	cabernet sauvignon, syrah, zinfandel, petite sirah	
PASTAS & GRAINS		
Pasta with Tomato Sauce or pizza	sangiovese, pinot noir, merlot, zinfandel, syrah, petite sirah	
Paella, Jamblaya	sangiovese, zinfandel, syrah, petite sirah	sauvignon blanc, pinot grigio, viognier
Cous-Cous, Quinoa, Risotto	pinot noir	sauvignon blanc, pinot grigio
POULTRY & FISH		
Chicken & Turkey	pinot noir, sangiovese	sauvignon blanc, pinot grigio
Duck & Goose	syrah, zinfandel	chardonnay
Hen, Quail, Squab, Rabbit	pinot noir, merlot	sauvignon blanc, pinot grigio
Delicate Fish	pinot noir	sauvignon blanc, pinot grigio, rosé
Firm Fish or Shellfish	pinot noir	chardonnay, pinot blanc, sauvignon blanc, pinot grigio, viognier
VEGETARIAN		
Sweetbreads	pinot noir	chardonnay, rosé
Eggplant	pinot noir, merlot	sauvignon blanc
Salads	pinot noir	sauvignon blanc
Quiche & Omelet		sauvignon blanc, pinot grigio, viognier
Soups	pinot noir	sauvignon blanc, pinot grigio

Chapter 5

I'm having
a breakthrough!

Encountering the Quandaries
and Joys of Wine with Food

Among the most frequently asked questions from friends and family over the years is the desperate what-do-I-serve-for-tonight's-dinner-party inquiry. My usual suggestion is to offer more than one choice of wine: either one white and one red, or one light-bodied red and one medium-bodied red. Beyond that, I need the specifics of the main course before naming wines. Even then, I don't promise perfect pairings with food but am confident they'll come close.

I'll never forget the moment a guest at a wine and food pairing I hosted in my home experienced his first perfect pairing. He shouted out loud, "I'm having a breakthrough!" It was the classic "ah-ha!" moment when a long struggle to understand something that once seemed foreign finally clicks, and concept becomes reality. My guest's breakthrough happened while enjoying one of wine-and-food's classic marriages—oysters with Muscadet, a light, tangy, dry white wine from the north Atlantic coast wine region at the western edge of France's Loire wine growing region.

He made his discovery by applying the first half of the oldest rule in wine and food pairing: drink white wine with fish, red wine with meat. Accordingly, he experimented with various white wines on hand, tasting each one with his oysters. If the extent of his wine and food pairing education ended before he hit upon his "epiphany wine," he would have been satisfied with "fair-to-good" pairings of his oysters with sauvignon blanc and chardonnay, but not comparable to the experience offered by the Muscadet. So, this golden rule was a starting point of an exploration that happened to end at the perfect destination. But following the golden rule doesn't always lead to a perfect pairing. In fact, sometimes it takes breaking the rule completely.

Wine and food pairing may be compared to matching components in your wardrobe. It's mainly a process that follows a set of guidelines, suggestions, and advice that point in the right direction and help avoid obvious disasters. While following these guidelines will improve your odds of enjoying wine with food, don't expect them to work every time. There are just too many variables and nuances inherent in wines, food ingredients, sauces, and cooking methods (not to mention personal preferences) that make that goal unachievable.

The process of finding great food and wine pairings is as enjoyable as it is educational, a search I eagerly resume almost daily at dinnertime. Two guidelines I use for exploring food and wine pairings are in the tables at the beginning of this chapter and in Appendix 4. Think of them like GPS devices pointing you in the direction of great food and wine pairings. Like GPS maps, however, you still need to keep your eyes open and trust your instinct at decision points. I estimate the guidelines will make at least 80% of your pairings quite satisfying and, on rare occasions, create a wine and food breakthrough moment.

30. How important is the pairing of wine with food?

Choosing your wine based upon how its style, flavor, and texture complement those in the accompanying dish increases the odds of experiencing a synchronous union of wine and food on the palate.

You might have wondered why pairing wine with food should pose a dilemma. After all, you know your favorite wine, so why not drink that with every meal? Well, you can—and you should—because lesson one in wine-food pairing is *your own personal wine preference overrides all other rules* If you absolutely love merlot, for example, and only merlot, then go ahead and drink it. In the craft of pairing wine with food, with all of its guidelines, rules, conditions, and exceptions, it is always acceptable to match your favorite wine with anything on your plate. If, however, you want the opportunity to experience marriages of food and wine that seem to be made in heaven, you may want to find a substitute for your merlot now and then.

Wine and food pairing is as much art as it is science. For example, instinct may tell you a red wine pairs with red meat. As it happens, it pairs technically speaking, as well. Tannin compounds in red wine physically link with fat compounds in the meat and work together as a palate cleanser. Don't worry, though. You don't need to know anything about the molecular composition of wine and food to find great pairings. In most cases, all it takes is a handful of tips pointing you in the right direction and some trial and error experimentation.

Wine and food pairing theory says wine should be treated just like food. It has flavor, weight, aftertaste, structure, and nuance. The process of matching a wine with a food, therefore, becomes a mind-numbing examination of countless possibilities as you consider all of their complexities and variables. But there is a clear place to start, at least: it's the age-old rule that says pair white wine with fish, red wine with meat. It may be passé with some sommeliers, but for quick, uncomplicated pairing decisions, it serves the purpose of launching you into subsequent decision points.

Once you apply the rule and choose either a white or red wine based on a fish or meat dish, respectively, you arrive at a fork in the road (sorry about that): which style of red or white wine do you choose? The answer, generally, is you choose a full-bodied wine with a robust dish and a light-bodied wine with a delicate one. After that, you take the decision tree to the next stage: you pair the dominant component of the wine with the dominant one in the dish. (If applicable, consider the structure of a wine, along with how a sauce or topping on the food might complicate a pairing. For example, a high-acidity white wine complements rich toppings like lobster sauce while a tannic red wine pairs well with grilled steak because both wines equalize the fat content in the paired dishes.)

When pairing dominant wine and food components, think about whether they complement each other because they are *similar* or because they *contrast*. Whichever direction you take, they should come together to create a palate sensation that neither the dish or wine could achieve alone. In other words, the food-wine "whole" should be greater than the sum of its individual parts.

Achieving perfect pairings of wine with food is rare, but you can optimize your wine and food experience and avoid obvious clashes by observing the suggestions in the tables at the start of this chapter, and in Appendix 4, and by observing the following guidelines:

- Pair the richness of the food with the mouthfeel of the wine: light-bodied wines for delicate dishes and full-bodied wines for rich food.

- Pair similar flavors in the wine and food—for example, a fruity wine for a dish topped with a fruity sauce—matching the fruit flavors as closely as possible.
- Pleasing combinations can be achieved by combining contrasting flavors—for example salty cheese paired with a sweet dessert wine.
- If you want to feature a very special wine, like an aged red wine, choose a "neutral" accompanying dish without bold flavors
- Dishes with vinegar, like salads, almost always make a wine taste bad. The best wine option is one with high acidity—maybe a sparkling wine, a dry riesling, or a French Beaujolais.
- It's perfectly fine to drink red wine with fish. Salmon pairs wonderfully with pinot noir.
- Choosing a wine that originates from the same country as the style of food improves your odds of creating a good combination. For example, choose a wine from Italy (or a domestic version of an Italian grape variety) to pair with Italian food.

Some classic food and wine pairings include: steak with cabernet sauvignon; lamb with either merlot or pinot noir; scallops or lobster with chardonnay; caviar with sparkling wine; Port-style dessert wine with salty Stilton cheese. Except for the last example, these classics happen to follow the old rule of red wine with meat, white wine with fish—*and* they match the weight, or mouthfeel, of the wine with the richness of the food. Thus, each creates harmony by matching either similar or contrasting components.

You experience a memorable taste sensation when a perfectly paired wine seems to meld with food on your palate. It may mean having to find a temporary substitute for your favorite wine, but it will be worth it. You'll recognize the magic the moment it happens.

31. Which wines are compatible with a wide variety of foods?

No single wine or wine style can pair perfectly with every dish, but pinot noir for red wine, and sauvignon blanc in the white wine category can cover more ground in the wine and food pairing landscape than any others.

Imagine yourself participating in a wine and food pairing game show. The drum rolls and your final question is to choose a wine—only one wine—for a group of four people about to eat dinner at a fine restaurant, and you have no knowledge of what dishes were ordered. Your objective is to choose a wine with the best odds of satisfying everyone at the table. This is almost always an impossible goal to achieve, not only because each person has their own preference in wine, but also because each has his or her own dinner selection, invariably bringing a wide variety of foods to the table. As the clock ticks down, what wine would you choose? While there are no "right" answers to questions of personal taste, your best final answer should be: pinot noir, if you choose a red wine; sauvignon blanc for a white wine.

In reality, the best way to approach this situation is to order both a white wine and red wine, especially when more than four people are having wine. Sauvignon blanc is versatile with almost any fish, vegetarian, and chicken dish because it's lightweight, delicately fruity, and crisp. It also tends to exhibit notes of freshly-cut grass, helping it pair well with salads, too. People who drink only white wine will feel comfortable if sauvignon blanc is the only option.

Choosing a red wine depends more on the overall style of food on the menu. If the choices are middle-of-the-road, bistro-style food with pastas, light meats, chicken, and light sauces, then a medium-bodied wine, such as pinot noir, will complement many of the nuanced dishes on the menu. Try pinot noir from Oregon, California, or France. As an alternative, try a sangiovese-based wine, like Italian Chianti, or else a Spanish or American tempranillo, an interesting Spanish grape with about the same mouthfeel as pinot noir and sangiovese.

If meat, game, and other big flavorful dishes and sauces dominate, a medium-to-full-bodied, blended red wine from any combination of grapes will probably handle the weight and intensity of most menu items. The specific varieties of the blend are not critical, but a Bordeaux or Meritage style blend of cabernet sauvignon with merlot is a good place to start. Or, try going with a cabernet sauvignon blended with syrah, or a merlot blend with sangiovese, both complex wines versatile with robust dishes.

When you are unsure of which wine, or wines, to order, whether for a large group or just for yourself, feel free to utilize the knowledge of the restaurant sommelier. His or her extensive training in wine, broad experience tasting countless wines, and familiarity with the dishes on the menu will take the pressure off you to make a quick decision and allow more time for you to enjoy conversation with dinner companions.

32. What wines match best with Asian cuisine?

If your preference is white wine, go crisp and light—and don't forget sparkling wine as an option. If in search of a red wine, steer clear of robust, highly tannic wines.

The popular Asian foods—Chinese, Japanese, Thai, and Indian— are usually paired with light-bodied white wines, served very chilled, either in a dry style or with a hint of sweetness. Crisp white wines blend nicely with the fish, vegetables, black pepper, spices, and stir-fried methods used in Asian foods. A mildly sweet riesling, with its flowery aroma and tingling texture, complements the saltiness of soy sauce and heat of wasabi. The gewürztraminer grape, from Germany and the neighboring Alsace region of eastern France, also has lightness and complexity that pair well with flavorful Asian dishes. Sparkling wines, the ultimate in lightness and acidity, meet the challenge with extra flair.

If red is your preference, there are light-bodied red wines that work well, but be careful not to choose one with very dry and firm tannin. It will clash with the delicate nature of many Asian foods. Red wines low in tannin are: sangiovese and barbera, made either in the U.S. or Italy; tempranillo, made either in the U.S. or Spain; Beaujolais, from France; and, once again coming to the rescue, pinot noir. Of course, if the dish is a spicy barbecued beef, include medium-bodied red wines in your options. Finally, a rosé wine, chilled slightly, either dry or a little sweet, is a great compromise when you can't decide which way to go with Asian-style foods.

33. Which wines are best for cooking?

You want quality in all of your cooking ingredients and wine is no exception. So, select wine for cooking with care equal to choosing one for consuming. Also, know that alcohol boils sooner than water and beware of wines labeled as "cooking wine."

Wine used in cooking loses much of its alcoholic strength as it is heated, leaving the remaining wine components to marry with those in the dish. The earlier in the cooking process wine is added, the more alcohol evaporates. Therefore, a splash of wine added near the end will retain more alcohol than a dose added at the start.

A recipe could call for texture, added by wine's acidity or tannin, or be enhanced by a grape's primary flavors that remain after alcohol evaporates. Part of the true varietal character of a grape variety is its primary flavor profile—present in every wine made by that grape. Use the primary flavors in the grapes below to support a recipe, either as similar-flavor or contrasting-flavor components:

- **Chardonnay**: green apple, pear, melon
- **Sauvignon Blanc**: herbal, vegetal, citrus

- **Pinot Noir**: red cherry, mushroom
- **Merlot**: blackberry, plum
- **Zinfandel**: blackberry
- **Cabernet Sauvignon**: blackcurrant, cassis, bell pepper

If you're thinking of using fortified wines like genuine Sherry, Port, Madeira and Marsala, be aware of their elevated alcohol content and know that some are made sweet and some are fully dry, so be sure you have the right style for your dish. Also, if you substitute wine for water in a recipe, remember to add cooking time to compensate for wine's lower boiling temperature; around 175°F versus 212°F for water.

Chefs who love wine as much as they love food believe any wine good enough to drink on its own is good enough to use in a recipe. You want a quality wine but it doesn't have to be expensive. For less than $10, you can find many good wines with style, flavor and depth. Put another way, if a wine does not appeal to you as a drink, it won't as an ingredient, either. Another bit of advice chefs give: don't use wines labeled as "cooking wine." These wines contain salt and do not have the complexity of flavor needed in an ingredient as vital as wine.

34. What wines pair best with Thanksgiving dinner?

Thanksgiving dinner is not the time to serve a wine of great finesse or delicacy. Too many of the side dishes—not to mention the savory roasted turkey—will probably overpower finely nuanced wines. Stronger red wines, preferably American made in keeping with the national holiday, better meet the challenge.

Thanksgiving dinner poses an interesting dilemma for the wine-pairing enthusiast. The breadth of flavors across the full meal—from roasted turkey to side dishes like sweet potatoes, vegetables, stuffing, gravy, and cranberry sauce—makes it impossible to pick one wine that complements everything. On the other hand, such a cornucopia offers plenty of opportunity to get at least one of them to match perfectly with the wine.

Since big food pairs well with big wine, look for a red zinfandel, syrah, or even petite sirah to stand up to Thanksgiving Day's weighty and flavorful menu. Zinfandel, by the way, is generally regarded as "America's grape," giving it an edge in a search for a wine to pair with this holiday. It has compelling, powerful qualities that don't get buried by an avalanche of flavors from this eclectic meal. Known for its jammy, dark berry flavor, exotic spice, and notes of black pepper, big red zinfandel can also have alcohol content as big as its flavor—sometimes as high as 18%.

If you want to also offer a white wine with Thanksgiving dinner, a chilled, dry riesling is versatile enough to pair adequately with many dishes. It's too light to cause any serious clashes and it cleanses the palate with refreshing acidity.

35. Which wines are best for barbecues?

Chilled white and rosé wines cool the palate but bold reds can take the heat—and sweet—of grilled meat smothered in barbecue sauce.

You may not think of wine as a thirst quencher, but a low-alcohol white wine, like pinot grigio, riesling, or even a rosé wine, can be quite refreshing in hot weather. This is one of two very different styles of wine good for summertime grilling. These wines are crisp, meant to serve chilled, and satisfying either in a dry or semi-dry wine. Beaujolais wines from France (*except Beaujolais Nouveau*) can also meet the need for a fruity, slightly chilled thirst quenching red wine to pair with a wide variety of summer dishes, including salads.

The other style to consider sits on the opposite end of the spectrum: it is a lush red wine, like syrah, grenache, zinfandel, or petite sirah. The sweet and spicy flavor in barbecue sauce—usually smothering grilled chicken or ribs—is compatible with the flavor intensity and full body of these wines. Both syrah and petite sirah have an exotic black fruit richness and spicy edge, but petite sirah is even darker than syrah and has an extra kick on the finish. Red zinfandel also delivers spicy fruit that works with grilled peppers and onions.

Finally, you can always break out the pinot noir when you need to satisfy many different palates. It can even work for a barbecued meal if the pinot noir is a full-bodied version. Some of California's Santa Barbara County pinot noirs can meet this need, handling grilled fish as well as mild red meats (but without the spicy hot sauces).

36. What foods match best with dessert wines?

Just as you pair dry table wine with dinner, you select a sweet after-dinner wine that matches the intensity, weight, and texture of the dessert. To enjoy a dessert wine to its fullest, make sure it is sweeter than the dessert.

While the main course has its "hall of fame" of food and wine pairings, the dessert course has its own legendary couples. One is sweet, Port-style wine paired with Stilton and other salty blue cheeses. It's an example of pairing contrasting components—sweet and salty—to create a wine-food marriage. Another contrasting component pairing teams up sweet and full-bodied Sauternes, from France, with salty Roquefort cheese.

Sauternes, a dessert in itself, is extremely expensive, especially from older vintages. It is handcrafted using only the best sémillon, sauvignon blanc, and moscadelle grapes available—shriveled on the vine from the Botrytis rot to almost raisin-like size, resulting in intense sugar concentration. It is produced only in years that meet the highest standards of Bordeaux's winemakers.

There's one pairing rule that puts sweet food with sweet wine, but this approach works only when the wine is sweeter than the food. Otherwise, the wine will taste flat and thin. Keep the relative weight of the dessert roughly equal to the weight of the wine: light dessert dishes work best with light, crispy white wines, like moscato. Heavier, richer desserts, filled with chocolate or draped in a sugar-heavy topping, need fuller-bodied sweet wines, usually red, like Late Bottled Vintage Port, Vintage Port and styles similar to them. Sometimes a full-bodied, sweet white wine, like Sauternes or Late Harvest riesling, will work, too. It just depends on your preference.

<u>Know It Like The Back of Your Hand</u>

Have you ever experienced a time when you were sipping away on a wine and taking a variety of small bites in between, but then noticed you weren't as pleased with the wine as when you took the first sip? Maybe you decided to try another wine, hoping it would taste better? Depending on what wine you switched to, and whether or not you continued eating, the change might have gotten your palate back on track. While it seemed to you the first wine changed, it actually didn't—it was the food that changed the wine.

I always placed food and wine pairing exercises towards the end of my wine tasting classes. I wanted people to experience the wines early, while their palates were fresh and untainted, because food can change the impression a wine gives on the palate. The objective in pairing any wine with food is to make that change a positive one—*when the food and the wine support and improve each other.*

The first exercise below demonstrates how food changes your impression of a wine. You may or may not feel it is a positive change, but you will notice a difference. In the second and third exercises you learn how to recognize similar-component and contrasting-component pairings. And in the final session, you experience a pairing that combines both similar and contrasting components in one.

I suggest taking each of the following four lessons on separate days to better focus on and learn from each experience.

- **Food Changing Wine**
  - Starting with a clean palate, take a few sips of chardonnay (preferably one without much oak). Take note of its apple and pear-like qualities and any impression of dryness or sweetness on your palate. Take your time. Get a feel for the wine and then take a bite of a medium-firm, mildly salty cheese, such as Manchego or Gruyere. Then, taste the chardonnay again. Ask yourself how the wine changed. Did it seem to taste sweeter on the second taste?
- **A Contrasting-Flavor Food Pairing With Wine**
  - Get a moscato, riesling, or sparkling wine *with sweetness* and pair it with a *salty* food—even a snack food, like popcorn or potato chips. Notice how each sip of wine after a taste of the salty food balances, quenches, and cleanses the palate.
- **A Similar-Flavor Food Pairing With Wine**
  - Pair fresh cherries (not maraschino) with pinot noir.
  - Pair a green apple with a dry riesling.
  - If you are feeling adventurous, try combining fresh oysters with a dry Muscadet wine from France, as my guest did when he had his wine and food pairing epiphany. (See the opening of this chapter.) Maybe you can replicate his breakthrough moment.
- **A Contrasting-and Similar-Flavor Pairing In One**
  - Pair petite sirah (*dry component*) with dark chocolate (*semi-sweet, contrasting component*). In addition, there are similar component flavors of cocoa in each.

How To Taste Wine Like A Pro

Observe	Examine the wine's color density and clarity. It can help indicate grape varietal, age, and whether or not the wine was filtered. Tilt the glass at an angle against a white background to get the best indication of the wine's true color.
Swirl	Swirling the glass will expose more wine to air and release vapors from the surface, making it easier for you to smell and identify aromas. (Decanting a wine in advance of drinking will also help release aromas.)
Sniff	Tilt the glass to expose a wider surface area of wine. Place your nose inside the glass and take one or two sniffs. Refer to Appendix 5 for help in identifying what the aromas resemble.
Taste	Swirl the wine inside your mouth and hold it for a few seconds. Practice taking in additional air to mix with the wine in your mouth. This will heighten the impact of the flavors on the palate.
Think	Concentrate on the flavors of the wine.
Spit	If you are evaluating many wines, spit the wine into a cup or container.
Evaluate	Refer again to the list of Aromas & Flavors in Appendix 5 to identify what you tasted and form your overall impression.

Chapter 6

My wife loves wine. She goes through a box a week.

Fine-Tuning Your Wine Appreciation

While dining with a colleague years ago, the subject of our conversation switched from engineering to wine. Naturally, my enthusiasm for wine surfaced and I eagerly asked about his preferences in wine. Almost instantly, that burst of energy deflated when he told me he was not a wine drinker—but it returned when he said his wife was a devoted fan. "My wife loves wine!" he said, followed by a pause, and the devastating follow-up: "She goes through a box a week. Keeps it in the refrigerator!"

I didn't ask if it was white or red.

There's a fine line between wine lover and wine snob. At the moment he told me his wife drank wine from a cardboard box, I stepped into the wine snob realm. A box of wine?! This worried me. But the moment flashed by so fast, I couldn't decide what bothered me more: that she was an avid fan of low quality wine or that I worked with the guy married to her! She turned out not to be the wine enthusiast I was hoping for, and though I tried hard to stop myself from showing disappointment, I couldn't contain my laughter.

Today, times are different—and I am, too! Boxed wine and jug wine, both viewed years ago as inferior quality wines, are now sources of decent inexpensive wine. One reason is that winemaking is significantly better today than it was decades ago, even for mass-production domestic and imported wines. Also, competition for the wine consumer has pushed prices of good wine downward and motivated producers to attract customers in new ways. Innovative packaging like cardboard boxes, plastic bottles, and aluminum cans help reduce prices, get attention, and address needs of a mix of lifestyles. These days I don't laugh at anyone drinking boxed wine—and I've even recommended boxed wine in my wine columns.

If you want to appreciate and learn more about fine wine, attend as many wine tastings as possible. When I started learning, I went to tastings at wine shops where the viewpoint of the retailer brought a unique perspective on wine values and consumer trends. Alternately, a wine tasting held at a winery (or at a restaurant, but hosted by a winery) provides insight into the brand's particular winemaking style, methods, and history. I've also attended wine tastings organized by distributors, historically, the middlemen in the wine-to-consumer transaction. They represent multiple wineries, from a handful to several hundred, depending on the size of the company and their market specialty, positioning them with an intimate understanding of the producer, retailer, and consumer.

Perhaps one of the best ways to taste new wines is at private home wine tastings, or even at your own home where you supply the wine or ask guests to bring a bottle. Each year, my wife and I conduct a blind wine tasting at our home and provide ten "mystery" (hidden labels) wines for a fun tasting and evaluation. We give it a central theme, for instance, a rieslings-only tasting, or California Bordeaux-style blends (Meritage wines). We wrap bottles with foil to cover labels and bottlenecks and number them one through ten. Guests vote for their favorites on a white board and, after a few hours of tasting (and eating), I reveal the labels after all votes are posted.

There are always surprises, especially if I throw in a ringer like I did once for a cabernet sauvignon-only tasting. Inserted into the mix of ten wines was a *12-year-old* bottle of Charles Shaw, also known as "Two-Buck Chuck." This wine rose to fame in 2001 when it started selling at a national grocery store chain for just $1.99 a bottle. Surprising everyone at that wine tasting, it scored fourth highest in votes!

There's a practical side to appreciating wine, too. After fighting a stigma for decades, screw caps (also called twist caps) are now used to close many bottles of fine wines, and in particular, white wines. Screw caps eliminate the ceremony of inserting a corkscrew, pulling the cork, and hearing the familiar, soft "pop," but they offer tremendous convenience in serving and storing wine, plus help preserve a wine's fruity freshness. (Their full benefits are explained in Question 20.)

There's one side of wine you could categorize as part traditional, part trendy. It's the preference for a wine glass designed for the specific grape variety you are drinking. There have long been customs for using different wine glass sizes and shapes for white wines, red wines, dessert wines, and sparkling wines, but there is a growing school of thought that varietal wines are presented at their best in their own "custom" glass, designed after years of exhaustive tasting trials and comparisons.

For example, cabernet sauvignon, pinot noir, and syrah are all medium- to full-bodied wines. Customarily, each is poured into the same type of medium- or large-bowl wine glass. But the varietal wine glass philosophy says these wines are enjoyed at their full potential when consumed from different glass shapes, each one designed to showcase a different wine varietal character. With precision, the varietal glass directs the nuances of the wine's aroma, flavor, acidity, or tannin to the consumer's nose, tongue, and palate.

I attended a demonstration of this at a wine tasting held by Riedel, probably the most recognized brand of wine glasses. I tasted wines served in a conventional wine glass, then re-tasted them in a glass designed for that specific wine. The difference was noticeable, but I was unsure if it was significant enough for every wine consumer to appreciate.

Varietal glass or not, I always look for the most appropriate wineglass at my disposal when I serve wine to guests—even if I pour it from the spigot of a cardboard box.

37. How do I learn to appreciate fine wine?

When you evaluate and compare a broad spectrum of single-varietal wines, it builds a core of wine knowledge. Taste with focus and frequency, and you eventually become more discriminating in your wine choices and more eloquent in their assessment.

Have you ever felt frustrated because you could not communicate exactly what you like or dislike in a wine? Do you have a hard time explaining what makes one wine better than another? Is "smooth" the only word you can think of to describe a pleasing wine?

Learning to appreciate the nuances that make an extraordinary wine distinct from an ordinary one is a process that can take years, depending entirely on how frequently one tastes and the scope of styles and price ranges tasted. Unfortunately, if you don't drink wine often, or seldom encounter the taste of fine varietal or blended wine, you don't build your mental database of wines and flavor profiles from which to draw and enable comparisons. This is understandable. There are more than 10,000 varieties of grapes around the world and the challenge for every wine lover is to experience as many of them as possible in one lifetime.

A university music instructor used to tell his students: "Practice makes perfect, but only if you practice perfectly." Because appreciating fine wine starts by building a mental database of wine, applying this philosophy sharpens the tools you need to construct it. It starts with practicing to recognize the true grape character of single-varietal wines before getting into the blends. Taste these wines on a regular basis and ask yourself each time, "Is it a true representation of the natural character of the grape variety?" Each time, make an entry in your memory bank of your impression of the wine. Over a period of time, you will have a solid foundation for appreciating fine wine.

There are some well-made and delicious wines on the market that ultimately fail the true varietal test. There is nothing wrong with these wines but they are not the best wines to use for building a mental database of true varietal flavor and aroma profiles. As your tasting experience grows you will also learn to recognize these exceptions when you taste them. To build your foundation properly—to practice perfectly—learn the components that form each grape's personality: color intensity, primary flavors, degree of sweetness or dryness, level of acidity, texture of tannin, and alcohol content.

Minor differences will invariably exist among wines made from the same grape variety because of differences in terroir and individual winemaking styles, but over time and many trials you'll learn what to expect from a merlot versus a pinot noir, for example. And you'll appreciate a pinot noir that tastes like pinot noir, not merlot.

As you get comfortable identifying true varietal character, start thinking about wine characteristics that might be a result of either winemaker intervention or the unique conditions of the wine appellation. Unless you talk with the winemaker or read the producer's wine notes, it is impossible to know for sure how one quality came to stand out more than another, but you still need to ask the questions that address the contrasts below:

- Balanced or unbalanced components—Do alcohol, tannin, acidity and fruit seem to create equal impact...or does one seem to stand out more than others?
- Lingering finish or short finish—Does the wine's impression disappear quickly after tasting...or does it remain on the palate long after?
- Powerful or mild—Does the wine bombard your senses of smell, taste and touch all at once...or does it seem like a more restrained and quiet stimulation?

- Lively or bland—Does it seem bright and active on your palate...or plain, almost watery or thin?
- Complex or one-dimensional—Do you sense more than one flavor and aroma...or does the wine bring little of interest to the palate?
- Elegant or plain—Does it combine softness of texture with a blend of interesting flavors and enticing aromas... or is it uninspiring, causing you to lose interest after the first or second taste?
- Smooth or coarse—Does the texture feel round, almost melting in your mouth...or does it seem chewy or dry?

Think of some other contrasts of your own. The descriptors you create will summarize how the producer and geographic peculiarities influence the wine. When you start recognizing these distinctions and forming your own critique, you raise your level of wine appreciation. You no longer drink wine—you *taste* wine. The next time you taste a cabernet sauvignon, for example, think back to your impressions of previous cabernet sauvignons. Ask yourself if your general impression is better, worse, or the same as the other cabernets. Start forming your own preferences, or dislikes, for the varietals, producers, regions, and wine styles that you experience.

With regard to fine wines, you can think of them as those wines made from one or more of the 31 grape varieties listed below. All are generally regarded as the "noble grapes" of the wine world, arguably responsible for the best wine in the world. The 31 varieties below are some of the 150 or so commercially grown varieties that fall under a specific European grape species called *Vitis vinifera*. Your exploration of wine will likely include exposure to most, if not all, of these 31 widely accessible grape varieties:

White Grapes

- **chardonnay**

- chenin blanc
- gewürztraminer
- grenache blanc
- marsanne
- muscat blanc
- pinot blanc
- pinot gris
- prosecco
- riesling
- roussanne
- sauvignon blanc
- sémillon
- viognier

Red Grapes

- barbera
- cabernet sauvignon
- cabernet franc
- gamay
- grenache
- malbec
- merlot
- mourvèdre
- nebbiolo
- petit verdot
- petite sirah
- pinot noir
- pinotage
- sangiovese
- syrah
- tempranillo
- zinfandel

With the convenient availability of wine online, it's probably possible to find wine made from any one of the 150 *Vitis vinifera* grapes, although many of them are not grown in the U.S. Those wines would have to be imported from various wine regions of the world.

38. What are the steps to tasting and evaluating fine wine?

Start with a clean palate and a clear glass. With focus and concentration, execute the four "s" words—see, smell, sip, spit (or swallow)—as you recall and compare previous experiences with similar wines. Form your opinion. Then ask the ultimate question: Is the wine worth the price?

Whether a wine professional is evaluating and scoring a wine, or a consumer is tasting for personal enjoyment and edification, the same senses are applied in the same sequence. Perhaps the only difference is that professional wine tasters will typically spit and not swallow their sips of wine because of the accumulated volume of wine tasted in the course of a workday. If you are a more serious wine enthusiast, know that it is not necessary to swallow wine in order to detect flavor. Also, morning is the time of day when taste buds are most sensitive. Just in case you were wondering.

The proper steps to wine tasting are easy to follow if you remember the four "s" words: see, smell, sip, and either spit or swallow. But first, proper preparation is vital if you want to give any wine a fair evaluation:

Preparing To Taste and Evaluate Wine At Home

Get a clear, unetched, 8-ounce wine glass, clean and free of musty odors or detergent smell and make sure that your own perfume or cologne also does not interfere with wine aroma. Also, get wines to their proper serving temperatures. (See Appendix 3.)

The room should be well lit—daylight the best, and all-fluorescent lighting the least favorable environment. Also, use a white tablecloth or napkin as a background for observing a wine's color through the glass.

You *must* begin your taste and evaluation with a neutral palate. This means not having strong residue from food, mints, gum, toothpaste, coffee, and candy—anything that can influence your impression of the wine. The single biggest cause of a wine getting a bad (often false) rap is a tainted palate. It makes the wine taste off, sometimes, awful. *Even a sip of beer or whiskey before tasting wine will hinder your ability to assess it fairly.*

Finally, when preparing to taste a series of different wine styles, organize them from left to right, starting with the lightest white wine and progressing to medium- and full-bodied white wines. Then, continuing to the right, arrange red wines, also from light-body to medium-body to full-body.

Examine Appearance & Aromas

Start every evaluation using your senses of sight and smell. Pour only enough wine to *fill about one-fourth to one-third of glass capacity*, tilt it about 45 degrees and observe the wine's appearance against a white background. Take notes on its hue, depth of color, edge (rim) color, and core (main body) color. Use this checklist to help identify what you see:

White Wine Colors

- Pale yellow or green
- Straw Yellow
- Yellow
- Deep Yellow-Gold
- Gold

Red Wine Colors

- Pale Red
- Brick Red
- Brownish Red
- Ruby Red
- Redish-Purple
- Purple
- Dark Purple

The body color of a young red wine is more purple than red. After a few years of age, color changes towards ruby-red, and with more age, say, 10 to 20 years or more, intensity of color lightens and the shade changes. It takes on a tinge of brown around the edge and sometimes the core, too. If a young red wine has a brown-tinted edge, it is likely an indication of a faulty, oxidized wine.

Changes in a white wine go in the opposite direction: the wine starts out with a pale, greenish hue and matures with a straw yellow tinge. As a white wine gets to around six years old, and older, its color gets darker and more golden. The degree to which a white wine takes on these changes varies with the grape variety. A chardonnay will become more golden over time than a sauvignon blanc, for example, but they will both undergo a darkening of color over time.

Any wine—red or white—is described as having good color intensity if it has density, or opaqueness, as you look through it. Color intensity is primarily a characteristic of the grape variety, due to either naturally darker color pigments on the skin or because of the size of the grape. Smaller grapes will generally produce darker wine because of their higher skin-to-juice ratio. But it's possible for color to be affected by the maceration period, controlled by the winemaker, or by weather just before harvest: some thin-skinned grapes subjected to heavy rainfall can become diluted, causing lighter-than-normal color intensity.

Finally, examine the wine's clarity by holding your glass toward a light source and looking for cloudiness. A white wine should be clear and bright. Some light should pass through a red wine, too, but without any visible particles creating a dull, cloudy effect. A bottle of red wine more than 10 years old may show a temporary cloudiness from normal sediment if agitated, but it is still okay to drink after decanting. Finally, if bits of cork appear, remove them with a spoon as they float to the top.

Smell The Wine in Two Stages

After color is observed, stick your nose in the glass and take two short sniffs. Note the fragrance intensity, or lack of intensity of this "static" aroma—in other words, before the wine has been aerated. Then, examine the intensity of the fragrance of the aerated wine—the "dynamic" aroma, after swirling it in small circles for about five seconds. (You can hold the stem of the glass with the base laying on a flat surface while swirling.) Swirling mixes wine with oxygen and helps bring out more aroma. Now, take another three to four short sniffs with your nose deep inside the glass. Is the dynamic aroma different from the static aroma? Did it become more intense? In most cases, swirling makes the wine more aromatic as exposure to more air helps the wine "open up."

After swirling and sniffing, think about whether the wine smells clean—in other words, it has no obvious faults. A bad wine with an off-smell will stick out immediately. You will rarely come across wines that have wine aroma faults, but it's good to be aware of them. If you do experience a faulty wine, it will likely be one of the following:

Wine Fault Aroma	Probable Cause
Musty, wet cardboard:	Indicates a bad cork from TCA contamination (See Question 41);
Caramel, cooked smell:	Wine was stored while exposed to excessive heat;

Gamey, animal, barnyard:	Wine was spoiled by an undesirable yeast strain (Brettanomyces, aka Brett) originating from grapes or an unsanitized barrel or piece of equipment (note: American winemakers do everything possible to avoid Brett, but European winemaking is tolerant of Brett in a small, controlled amount.);
Nail polish remover:	An undesirable yeast spoiled in the wine;
Rotten egg:	Insufficient nitrogen in fermentation
Sulfur, burnt match:	Over-application of sulfur dioxide;
Sour, "sherried" smell:	Excessive oxygen spoiled the wine;
Vinegar	Bacteria spoiled the wine

If nothing in the aroma seems out of the ordinary, ask yourself if the aroma is typical of its true grape varietal. For example, if you are evaluating a pinot noir, does it have the familiar aromas of red and black cherries and maybe a hint of mushroom? If you are not familiar with the typical characteristics of the grape, simply concentrate on what comes to mind while referring to the quick-reference table in Appendix 6.

Technically speaking, grapes alone are responsible for aroma while *bouquet* is the more complex fragrance that develops as a result of aging. However, it is not unusual—or poor wine etiquette—to use them interchangeably. And while the bouquet of some wines might entice and maybe even indicate flavor, it will not foretell structure, alcohol, and balance. Surprises often happen, some positive, some negative, after the first sip is taken. *Wine with weak aroma intensity does not indicate it will have mild flavor or little power; by the same token, a wine with strong aroma intensity does not portend a big-alcohol, or flavorful wine.*

Taste The Wine

Sip about an ounce of wine and swish it around in the mouth. You can also attempt to simultaneously suck in some air—actually, slurping—in order to mix even more oxygen with the wine and bring more flavor to the palate. (This takes some practice.) Concentrate on your first impressions of flavor and texture. Spit out the wine into a separate cup or container.

Think first in broad terms, and then narrow down your impressions. Some broad questions first:

- Is the wine **light-bodied** (thin, almost a watery feel), **medium-bodied** (about the same weight as milk), or **full-bodied** (heavy, or viscous, like cream)?
- Is it filled with a single dominant flavor or is it complex with a multitude of flavors?
- Does the fruit jump out, or is it subtle? Does it seem masked by other components?
- Is the wine approachable and easy to drink, or does it seem out of balance? Is the alcohol content in balance with other components?
- Does it have any detectable sweetness or does it seem completely dry?
- Is the texture crisp (like apple juice) or soft and round (like milk)?

Sip again and narrow down your impressions further:

- If tasting a red wine, is the fruit light, like cherry, or a more concentrated dark fruit, like black cherry or blackberry?
- Is there an impression of dryness from tannin that makes the mouth pucker? Is the tannin so dry that it hampers your ability to taste anything or does it support the fruit?

- Does the wine have any flavor imparted by oak barrels, such as vanilla, coconut, toasted bread, or char? Does that flavor complement the wine or does it overpower the fruit?

Although industry professionals generally apply commonly used descriptive wine terms for aromas and flavors, feel free to use whatever words come to you and use the quick-reference table in Appendix 5 to trigger your mind to identify the components you detect.

After another sip and spit, think about the wine's **finish**.

- How fast does the wine's impression fade after swallowing, or spitting? Does it disappear instantly or linger? Is it pleasing enough to invite you to taste again? The best wines in the world often finish slowly and leave a delicious impact on the palate that leaves you wanting more.

There are no right or wrong answers—your own impressions count more than what others think.

Draw Your Conclusions

After observing, smelling, and tasting, what conclusions can you draw about the wine?

- Is it pleasing, but ordinary?
- Is it unique and well-balanced, but not your style?
- Is it delicious, but possibly difficult to pair with food?

The Value of Wine

Many questions come out of a wine tasting, but the ultimate question is: *"Is it worth the price?"* No matter how much you may enjoy a particular wine, final assessment always comes down to value, which is subjective and personal: like many luxury items, the higher the price, the greater the expectation. On rare occasions, expectations are exceeded, like when a $12.00 bottle of chardonnay presents itself like a $30.00 bottle, or better. To notice such value, one needs to devote the time to taste many chardonnays at different prices to recognize and appreciate the discovery.

Experiencing a wide variety of wines, however, can get expensive, especially if you are purchasing bottles just for tasting purposes—and without any certainty you'll even like the wine! But it is a fun part of the exploration into wine. Attend as many wine-tasting events as possible, both private and public, that offer multiple wines at a single event. It makes your self-education more cost-effective.

Try not to get stuck repeating the same styles, regions, or producers all the time. Make a conscious effort to taste uncommon grape varieties, different wine styles, a mix of domestic and imported wines, and new and unfamiliar brands, all in an effort to keep your wine awareness level current and broad. It helps avoid a palate rut that tends to only appreciate a narrow range of wines. It sometimes requires paying a little more for wine than you might be accustomed to, but it broadens your wine horizon. It all contributes towards building your personal definition of wine value.

Another conclusion you might draw from a wine evaluation is whether or not you would recommend the wine to friends. You might like a wine and its value and suggest it to others, but it's hard to predict their standards or value expectations. There will always be some wines that you recommend that others will reject, along with some that you reject that will be perfectly fine with others.

Finally, before you move to the next wine in your home tasting, drain previous wine from the glass. Before you move from white wine to red, either rinse the glass with water or use a new glass. Cleanse your palate in between wines with water or neutral crackers or bread.

39. How do I conduct a wine tasting at home?

Come up with a tasting theme and then decide either to assign each guest a wine to bring or to provide the wines yourself. Covering labels adds intrigue and suspense to the event, whereas keeping them visible allows direct comparisons of appellations or producers as tasting progresses.

Wine-themed parties and dinners are a great way to explore new wines while socializing with others who enjoy wine as much as you do. While a sit-down, wine tasting dinner has courses that pair with specific wines, a casual wine tasting party does not necessarily have to include dinner, but some food should be available.

Decide first on a theme. You could create a pinot noir tasting, for example, and assign a different pinot noir appellation to each guest. In other words, one guest has to bring a Santa Barbara pinot noir, another an Oregon pinot noir, another from Sonoma, and so on. Pick a vintage that is still readily available (usually released within the last three years). Guests can choose any producer and price level they want, but it's a good idea to establish a price range. Or, you could provide all the wines yourself. In either case, be sure there will be enough wine for everyone to taste 1 to 3 ounces of each wine.

Once deciding on a theme, plan for having food that pairs with the wines. You can keep things simple with just bread, crackers, and a variety of cheeses and cold meats. Or, be daring and experiment with a range of small dishes, hot and cold, allowing guests to seek out perfect pairings. If you choose a theme that results in a broad selection of wines—for instance, white and red wines from Paso Robles, vintage 2010—you're bound to find a few great pairings among all the possible combinations.

Bottles should be placed in full view on a main table for guests to pour for themselves. Hand everyone a glass and remind them to take small samples so that the wines get distributed as evenly as possible. Alternatively, you can get pouring control tops for wine bottles that limit the volume of each pour.

Another approach is a "blind" wine tasting where guests don't know what they are tasting because bottles are wrapped in paper bags or foil and labels are covered. Each guest arrives with their pre-assigned bottle already inside a bag that hides everything but access to the cork. Assign guests a number and have them write it on the outside of the bag, easy for people to see.

Once all wrapped wines are numbered and arranged on the table, give guests only one hint about the wines: red wines are in one area, white wines in the other. That's all they should know. The varietal, brand, style, or appellation of each wine should remain unknown to everyone, except, of course, to the person who brought it.

Allow a couple of hours for everyone to taste all the wines, pair them with food, and rate each one from 1 to 10 on a personal scorecard that you create and hand out in advance. Then take everyone's scores (make sure each card has the guest's name), total them for each wine, and announce the top scoring wines of the night. Return each person's card so each guest can compare the score he or she gave with the scores of the best wines of the party. You can create categories for best white wine, best red wine, even worst wine. The most exciting moment comes next, when you remove the bags and reveal the labels.

40. What is corkage? Is it okay to bring my own bottle of wine to a restaurant?

Some restaurants—and some states—restrict you from carrying in and consuming your private bottle of wine in a restaurant. Check ahead, and if their policy is open, remember to use proper "carry-in wine etiquette." Bringing your own wine can save you some money, even after paying for the privilege via a corkage fee.

A wine list that is either too limited or overpriced—or both!—may motivate you to pack a bottle of your own on subsequent trips to the restaurant. Another reason could be the wine list is geared toward mass-produced, national brands or lacking a variety of styles. This is not implying that wine by a national brand is not good. But some of these big names seem to be everywhere and sometimes you just want a special bottle of wine to make the occasion more memorable. If you're thinking of bringing your own wine to a restaurant, keep these tips in mind:

- If you are uncertain about the restaurant's policy, call in advance or check its website to find out. Some restaurants don't permit private party wine, a restriction more acceptable if their wine list is extensive, diverse, and reasonably priced.
- Choose a wine that is special. In other words, don't bring an ordinary supermarket brand that is available everywhere. If possible, avoid bringing a bottle the restaurant already has on its list—many restaurants publish their wine lists on their websites. To be safe, choose an older vintage they are less likely to offer.
- Expect to pay a restaurant charge, known as **corkage**. This pays for the server opening and pouring your wine and providing a bucket for keeping a white wine chilled. Corkage usually ranges from $5.00 to $25.00, depending on the restaurant. Some waive this fee if another bottle is also ordered from the wine list.
- As a courtesy, offer a taste to either your server, restaurant manager, or sommelier. It is always appreciated, especially if you bring an older wine, or one from a little-known, high-quality producer.
- Tip your server based upon your dinner price plus the approximate value of the wine you brought.

41. What is a corked wine?

A corked wine, tainted by an unappealing smell of dampness, is the winemaker's public enemy number one. Though this flaw frequently goes unnoticed by the average wine consumer, the wine industry is taking steps to reduce and ultimately eliminate corked wines forever.

A corked wine is not what it sounds like. It is not wine that has pieces of broken cork floating inside the bottle or one that is oxidized because a dry cork failed to adequately seal the bottle. Rather, a corked wine has been tainted—in the worst cases, completely ruined—by a cork that contains a chemical called **TCA**. It's instantly recognizable by its musty, damp, wet cardboard smell. It is an odor obvious to anyone who makes, sells, or recommends wine for a living, but one which might get past consumers depending on its intensity.

When the taint is subtle, the wine remains drinkable. But in the worst cases, it is hard to even stick your nose in the glass. Though it's not harmful if a corked wine is consumed, the problem is in its power to destroy fruit fragrances the winemaker took great effort to produce and protect. This is the primary reason why many in the winemaking industry feel an urgency to move to alternative methods of bottle closures, including twist caps, which have zero chance of contaminating a wine with TCA. (See Question 20.)

42. What do wine nose, legs, and body mean?

The "nose" of a wine entices with fragrance, while the "legs" tease, and the "body" shows voluptuousness. These terms are shorthand expressions for what is sniffed, observed, and felt by the wine taster. File these words under the category of "wine lingo." They are uttered by collectors, competition judges, and wine shop managers as often as winemakers and critics. They are "wine code" for what our senses detect in the examination and evaluation of wine.

Nose is the wine world's synonym for smell. A wine is said to have an attractive nose if it has a noticeable, distinctive, and pleasing aroma that invites the taster to indulge. Wine with a poor or weak nose has little to no aroma, or has a noticeable fault. A wine with a faint nose may only need time to open up, something that a few swirls of the glass or a few minutes of aeration might resolve. Because our sense of smell is responsible for about 80% of what we appreciate in wine, a wine's nose is its most impressionable component. However, a light nose is not an indication of a lack of flavor or strength, and a boldly aromatic nose is not necessarily a sign of a big, powerful wine.

Once you stop swirling the glass and hold it steady, the dripping streams of wine clinging to the inside wall of the bowl and falling back into the wine are wine **legs**. Although there is some speculation as to the value of observing wine legs, they are generally regarded as visual indicators of richness. While exceptions always exist, most high alcohol wines exhibit wide, slow moving legs. The legs of lighter wines tend to be narrow and drip down more rapidly.

Finally, our sense of touch is applied when a wine's **body** is assessed. Also known as **mouthfeel**, body describes how a wine weighs on the tongue and overall palate. Wines with light body, like riesling, give a fresh, delicate feeling on the palate, made possible from a combination of relatively high acidity and low alcohol content. Most white wines and sparkling wines fall into the light-bodied category.

Full-bodied wines sit on the opposite end of the wine body spectrum, exhibiting noticeable weight on the tongue, bathing your palate with unmistakeable volume. As you would expect, full-bodied wines, red or white, tend to have deeper color and higher alcohol content, including viscous, golden-hued chardonnays with alcohol around 13.5% or more. Medium-body wines, in red or white, will have a mouthfeel that falls between light- and full-bodied. Examples are pinot noir for red, sauvignon blanc for a white wine.

As it happens, the vast majority of red and white wines can be described as medium bodied—not exactly lightweight and crisp but far from lush and heavy, either. Cabernet sauvignon and merlot may fall into either the full- or medium-body category, depending on where the grapes were grown and the manipulation of the wine by the winemaker.

43. Why do wineglasses come in a variety of shapes?

From the second you stick your nose in the glass to the moment a wine comes to a savory finish, an optimally designed vessel for that specific wine helps focus and deliver its full potential in aroma and flavor to the taster.

Just as the proper serving temperature presents a wine's best qualities, so does a properly shaped wine glass. The philosophy is simple: the content inside the glass determines the shape of the bowl. And for each wine style, from light and crisp white wines to full-bodied, high-alcohol reds, there is a wine glass to fit the need—right down to the specific grape variety.

The following breaks down glass bowl shapes according to three styles of wine—sparkling, white and red. For a detailed explanation on how a bowl shape and size changes for specific grape varieties, go to Riedel.com:

- **Sparkling Wines:** Although this category has the most variation in bowl shape, the most common are tall and narrow bowls, most too small to plunge your nose into and swirl the wine but still able to highlight a delicate bouquet. It also allows bubbles to hit the surface with greater fizz than in a wider, shallower glass, make them last longer, and stimulate the palate with a more sparkling sensation.
- **White Wines:** Not as narrow as a sparkling wine bowl. For full-bodied white wine, like chardonnay, the

inward-curving rim focuses the wine at the middle of the tongue where the bulk of its weight is welcomed. For lighter, fresher white wines, such as riesling, a French Chablis, pinot grigio, or sauvignon blanc, the rim of the bowl curves outward to direct wine to the tip and sides of the tongue to emphasize fruit and acidity.

- **Red Wines:** A glass for light- to medium-bodied red wines, like pinot noir, has a slightly wider bowl than the full-bodied white wine glass but with the same outward-slanting rim to deliver acidity to the edges of the tongue and allow fruit to be detected first. Full-bodied, tannic red wines, like cabernet sauvignon, need a large-diameter bowl to create a wide surface area that exposes a maximum amount of wine with air and allows greater swirling and aeration. Its inward-curving rim delivers a bounty of acidity, fruit, and tannin in balance to the middle of the palate.

44. What's the best way to save an unfinished wine?

With a suitable closure and a cool environment, you can preserve a partially vacant bottle of red wine overnight without worrying about spoilage. Place it inside a refrigerator for added measure or longer term storage.

The simplest way to save any wine is to re-cork it and keep it cool until next time. If the cork has broken or punctured through the full length, you will need to find a substitute closure, like a relatively clean, unbroken cork saved from another bottle, or a reusable silicone wine bottle closure. Essentially, you need a closure that seals the bottle opening well—maybe not perfectly, but good enough for the short term. Of course, if the bottle has a twist cap closure, you're good to go.

If you want to preserve a red wine, and you plan to pour from this bottle the very next day, re-close it and leave it on your kitchen counter, under the condition that room temperature will not rise above 70°F over the course of the next 24 hours. If it will, store the bottle in the refrigerator. Naturally, if it's a white wine, you'll want to store it the refrigerator regardless of when you plan to serve it again.

The next day, the red wine left at a cool room temperature will taste as good as it did the first night—maybe even better. Some wines noticeably improve with just a little exposure to air, like the amount it gets from the open space inside a partially-filled bottle. If your wine happens to be one of them—and there's no way to know for sure which ones will improve significantly—the "second edition" of the wine will be a nice treat.

But let's say you aren't exactly sure when you will pour again from this bottle. In this case, refrigerate the wine (red or white) after re-closing it and you can be certain it will be good for the next two days and maybe more. Refrigeration slows the aging process and keeps the wine relatively fresh, but it doesn't improve much in the refrigerator. After day two, a gradual decline in quality through the slow process of oxidation will be noticeable. Remember, the closure you used to re-seal the bottle is not perfectly air-tight. Some microscopic amounts of air will creep into the bottle.

There are tools on the market designed to keep unfinished wine fresh overnight, even without refrigeration, as long as the wine's environment stays below 70°F. (Around 60°F is ideal.) One product pumps the air from the bottle through a tiny slit on the top of a custom, pump-compatible rubber closure. This product works well and will extend the life of the wine longer than just re-corking the bottle, saving it for up to ten days, depending on the wine and how much air is in the bottle. Again, refrigeration adds an extra level of confidence to the process.

The other product is a gas canister filled with harmless and odorless argon gas. You place a thin, tubular spout through the neck of the bottle, press a button at the top (like you would on a can of spray paint), and send a blast or two of gas into the bottle.

The gas pushes out oxygen and replaces it, helping to preserve the wine. You then quickly seal the bottle with a suitable closure before letting the gas escape. It works great. For added safety, refrigerate the wine, too. Wine will remain fresh for at least a week, even months, according to the manufacturer.

45. What are the proper conditions for storing wine?

Put simply, warm environments hasten wine's aging while cool environments slow aging; and exposing a wine to extremes in temperature—high or low—must be avoided at all times.

If you typically consume your wine purchases within a month or so, the storage environment is important, but not as critical as it is if you lay away your wine for long-term storage and aging. In either case, you should protect your investment by applying some basic guidelines below:

- Once wine is damaged by heat, it is destroyed forever. Beyond the danger zone of 75°F, wine begins to break down chemically, damaging its integrity and composition. Even storing wine bottles in environments where temperatures are consistently above 70°F should be avoided. Planning a summer tour of wine country? Be sure to avoid leaving precious wine purchases in the trunk of your car!
- At the other extreme, the lowest temperature for your storage area should be about 45°F. If your wine is exposed to extremely low temperatures—below 40°F—it slows aging and could produce crystal-like particles (potassium tartrates) that accumulate on the cork or at the bottom of the bottle. A storage room kept between 50°F and 60°F is ideal, allowing wine to age at a normal rate and reach its prime with full potential to inspire.
- Humidity is not as critical as temperature, although it is generally targeted at 70% to 75% for home wine cellars.

If humidity is consistently above 90%, and your wines are in wooden crates, mold may eventually show up on the wood or on the tops of any corks unprotected by a metallic capsule.

- Storing bottles on their sides will keep wine in contact with the cork and ensure that it remains moist and expanded, keeping a tight closure against the glass. A dry cork, caused by a bottle stored upright for too long, will become brittle, shrink, and allow too much air to get to the wine.

If you become a serious wine collector, consider getting a wine storage unit that looks and works similar to a normal refrigerator. It often comes with sliding shelves, precision control of temperature and humidity, a low light environment, vibration-damping design, and a clear glass door. Available in a variety of sizes holding as few as 24 bottles or as many as 2000-plus, the largest are walk-in "rooms" complete with lights, racks, shelves, and refrigeration unit, delivered ready to assemble.

In apartments, or houses without basements, a wine storage unit is almost a necessity for keeping valuable wines. However, if you have a house with a basement or underground space with a fairly consistent temperature throughout the year, you automatically have a low-cost, convenient wine cellar. Always keep wines in a relatively dark area, too, as sunlight and, to a lesser extent, fluorescent light will harm delicate wines.

46. Why is white wine served colder than red wine?

A red wine served at normal room temperature, rather than chilled, is more aromatic and shows softer, more pleasing tannin. White wines need chilling to feature its higher acidity. If served too warm, they taste flat and bland.

Did you ever notice how a fine piece of art or jewelry always looks better under a spotlight? While proper lighting brings out the best in art, poor lighting diminishes the likelihood that you will see all of its beauty. Think of wine the same way: serving temperature impacts wine as much as lighting impacts art.

A wine's best features are brought out when served at the proper temperature. For example, light white wines with high acidity and refreshing crispness, such as riesling or pinot grigio, are best served at around 46°F to 50°F—almost as cold as a sparkling wine is served. Chilling brightens acidity, giving it a palate-cleansing quality, like whisking water off a car windshield. If you serve white wine too warm it becomes flat, dull, and unappealing.

Full-bodied white wines, like oak-fermented chardonnay or pinot blanc, taste better with slightly more warmth, around 50°F to 54°F, allowing more potent aromas of these grapes to come forward. It's unfortunate, but too often restaurants and bars serve chardonnay, and even lighter-bodied white wines, too cold, which suppresses the wine's bouquet. (You can speed up raising the temperature of the wine by cupping your hands around the bowl of the glass.) Also, if you are served a bottle too cold, don't bother to have the server place it in an ice bucket. Just leave it on the table to allow it to warm up to the proper temperature.

While chilling a white wine brings out its acidity, a chilled red wine high in tannin will taste bitter and harsh, like hot tea tastes after it has cooled—too dry and hard to drink. One red wine exception is French Beaujolais. Its bright fruit and high acidity show better when slightly chilled. Other light- to medium-bodied red wines with some acidity, like sangiovese or pinot noir, need a little more warmth and are best when served around 60°F to 62°F. More robust red wines like cabernet sauvignon, merlot, zinfandel or syrah are best served closer to 65°F in order to bring their heavy-duty aromas forward and soften the impact of tannins. See the quick-reference table in Appendix 3 for a breakdown of all wine serving temperatures.

47. When is it necessary to decant wine?

Part ceremonial, part practical, you decant a red wine for the purpose of aeration or to separate it from sediment, or both. The older the wine, and the more handcrafted the quality of its production, the more expressive it becomes after decanting.

In the course of going through a bottle of red wine—or sometimes even in the time it takes you to finish one glass—have you ever noticed the wine improving? Perhaps more aromas are detected, or the finish lasts longer. That's because the wine is getting aerated, also called "**opening up**," and releasing its full potential in aroma, flavor, and texture.

Decanting is the transfer of a red wine from its bottle into a new container, either for the purpose of aeration or to separate wine from its **sediment**, or sometimes both. For aerating purposes, decanting hastens the mixture of air and wine, a good idea for some young aromatic red wines that get more expressive when aerated. Alternatively, you can also aerate wine by giving it time in the glass before consuming. The unique shape of a decanter—wide at the bottom, tapering up to a skinny neck—allows more rapid aeration than simply uncorking the bottle. The decanter exposes a large surface area of wine to air and releases more of the wine's fragrant aromas.

After pouring from bottle to decanter, let the wine stand in the decanter for at least 20 minutes before pouring the wine into glasses. Keep in mind, old wines lose their aromatic power quickly, so *decant very old wines minutes, not hours, before serving.* If you wait too long before pouring, you will miss much of the wine's complexity and aromatic detail.

Decanting also separates wine from sediment that forms over time. Red wines of significant age, and some young ones, may show black sediment at the bottom of the bottle, or clinging to its side. It isn't a fault in the wine. It's a natural residue from phenolic compounds—tannin molecules combining with color pigments.

Or, crystal-like particles of sediment, from potassium or calcium tartrates, might show up in the bottle. Although, there's no harm in drinking wine with either sediment, it isn't pleasant. It's worth taking the extra step to decant in order to enjoy the wine without the bitterness of sediment.

To decant older wine that contains sediment, first allow the bottle to stand undisturbed for about 24 hours in advance of opening, if possible, to allow the solids to settle. Shaking the bottle before uncorking will stir up sediment and make decanting more difficult.

To uncork an old vintage, pull the cork gently—don't twist—to avoid breaking it. Then, pour it slowly into a decanter while simultaneously observing the wine passing through the neck of the bottle. As soon as sediment is visible through the neck, immediately stop pouring. To make it easier to see the wine the instant the particles are visible, place a lit candle under the neck or hold a flashlight against it, as many sommeliers do. You will likely end up with a few ounces of wine and sediment remaining in the bottle.

If you prefer to decant every red wine, regardless of age, clarity, or quality, there is certainly nothing wrong with that. With complex red wines that feature layers of fruit and receive extended oak aging, decanting will ensure that you get everything the wine has to offer. It's a small step that adds big to the enjoyment of wine.

48. What is the proper way to open and serve sparkling wine?

The high pressure inside a bottle of sparkling wine requires more care than pulling a cork from a bottle of still wine. Make sure the bottle is chilled properly, the cork does not twist as it is pulled, and a towel traps the cork and any wine as they spring from the bottle.

Don't let the extra effort involved with opening a bottle of sparkling wine keep you from experiencing one of life's great palate pleasures. You only need to remember that the secret to a safe and proper cork-popping is all in the wrist.

To get started, make sure the bottle is properly chilled to 40°F to 45°F. Aside from losing its crisp, refreshing nature, a warm sparkling wine will have an expanded volume of carbon dioxide gas trapped inside the bottle that will create extra foaming when released, causing a loss of wine. If you need to chill a bottle quickly, fill a bucket with ice and water and stick the bottle inside for about 15 minutes.

Remove the foil wrapping on the top of the neck, and expose the wire cage that surrounds the cork. Because the pressure inside a sparkling wine bottle is an impressive 80 to 100 pounds per square inch, take the following steps to protect yourself and others from a cork that might unexpectedly eject from the bottle as soon as you begin untwisting the wire. Place a towel over the neck of the bottle before you loosen the wire tab. Twist it counter-clockwise four to five times and either remove the wire cage entirely or leave it fully loosened. Then, with your palm facing up, grab the cork with the towel. It will slow the cork if it ejects from the bottle, and catch any wine that might spill out. Hold the fat part of the bottle in your free hand while gripping the cork with the towel hand and applying a little pressure with your thumb on top of the cork. *Slowly turn the bottle only with your wrist—do not turn the cork as it inches its way out.* Continue to hold the cork with the towel until it is completely out of the bottle.

You may be tempted to pull the cork, which is normal since we open bottles of still wine by pulling on the cork with a corkscrew. With sparkling wines, twisting just the bottle reduces the chance of breaking the cork and permits greater control of the cork as a dangerous projectile. You'll know if you opened the bottle properly if you hear a soft, muffled "pop" rather than a sharp, loud "crack". The softer the "pop", the more you preserved carbon dioxide gas, which is what creates the precious bubbles!

Pour only enough sparkling wine to fill half of a tall fluted or tulip-shaped glass. Wait for the initial rise of bubbles to subside, then pour slowly again until about 90% of the glass is filled. Then place the bottle in an ice bucket to keep it chilled.

Think about serving sparkling wine on any occasion, not only for special events and celebrating the new year. It's perfect to hand out as you greet arriving guests, as an apéritif before dinner, or with fresh fruit for dessert. So many different foods can be paired with sparkling wine, from oysters and light hors d'oeuvres to mild cheeses and popcorn. It takes only a little more effort to get started with sparkling wine, but you and your guests will always appreciate it.

49. Do you have any suggestions for giving wine as gifts?

First, match the recipient's lifestyle to a wine style; then choose a wine from a small, maybe even a local, producer. Quality generally increases with price, but differences become noticeable beyond a 20% price spread.

With wine, generally you will get a higher quality as you pay more, but the jump in price has to be significant, say, more than 20%. Prices differences within 20% of each other will probably not make noticeable differences in quality. If you know little or nothing about the gift recipient's specific wine preferences, try choosing a wine based on his or her personality or lifestyle. Here are some ideas:

- **Champagne and Sparkling Wines**: Safe as a gift at any time. They symbolize celebration, happiness, good times, and also serve as a pre-dinner beverage. The original sparkling wine, French Champagne, tends to be the most expensive sparkling wine (major brands start at around $25) while American sparkling wines made in the French traditional method are more affordable—and many are just as good. If you prefer to give a more affordable imported sparkling wine, look for Italian Prosecco or

Spanish Cava—they usually come at lower prices than French Champagne.

- **Pinot Noir:** An extremely nuanced wine, but also a versatile wine that is appreciated by devotees of both red and white wines. Pinot noir tends to cost a little more, on average, than other varietal wines, so expect to spend more than $25 if you want something of quality and true varietal character. Choose a wine from a small AVA in either California or Oregon, or from New Zealand.

- **Cabernet Sauvignon or Merlot:** Two classic, medium- to full-bodied, single-varietal wines appropriate for someone who tends to be more traditional in their food selections—perfect for the meat-eater. Choose a sub-appellation of either Napa or Sonoma Valley in California, from the Columbia Valley in Washington, or the Coonwarra region of Australia. American Meritage blends are also good options. Expect to pay $20 and up for Meritage or single-varietal wines.

- **Bordeaux or Burgundy, white or red:** A good choice for the scholar of world history, or lover of European culture. Also, for someone who frequents fine restaurants in big cities, entertains guests or clients, or dabbles in gourmet cooking. (These are not wines to use *in* cooking!). Pricing, on average, will be higher than domestic wines from comparable varietals, but that won't go unnoticed by the recipient. Prepare yourself to pay at least $30 for a bottle.

- **Chianti:** Nothing says "amore" better than an Italian red wine from the heart of Tuscany. Furthermore, if you upgrade your selection to the category of Chianti *Classico* (a small, sub-appellation of Chianti) the gift says you pay attention to detail. For the very special person, however, look for the *Riserva* term on the label—it indicates the wine was aged in barrel longer than non-Riserva wine, adding to its harmonious taste and romantic symbolism.

Always a great gift for anyone who loves Italy and Italian food.

Another gift-giving approach is to choose a wine that has some personal meaning to you. Because today, remarkably, every American lives in a wine-producing state, you can give a wine from your state if your recipient is from out of state. And, because most of these wineries are small, they typically won't have nationwide distribution, which reduces the chance the recipient will already have the same wine. Or, give a wine from producers you've personally visited. The wine has more meaning if a story about your personal experience is behind it.

50. How do I start a wine collection?

A great wine collection puts more emphasis on including a variety of styles over expensive wines. And it must take into consideration your wine lifestyle, entertaining frequency, and culinary choices as much as your personal wine preferences.

You've got the wine "bug" if you increasingly enjoy wine, discovering new favorites, and exploring different wine styles. You may have started to think about building a collection of wines at home. Like every other hobby, you can go at it with a budget that is tight or unlimited, or somewhere in the middle. What matters more than the amount you spend on a wine collection is the diversity of wines in the collection.

A wine cellar—any space you devote to wine storage—does not have to include expensive, rare, or even old vintage wines. It first has to satisfy your own taste preferences and enable pairing with your most frequent choices of dishes. Also, stock up on "safe" wines that have wide appeal to many palates. This makes it easy to please guests whose wine preferences are unknown.

Rather than chasing down a list of specific wines for your cellar, build your collection around popular wine *styles*. It doesn't matter whether you spend an average of five dollars or fifty dollars a bottle to start the collection; what's important is to have each of the categories below represented so you have wines available to address any situation. The number of bottles your cellar includes for each style depends on your budget, how often you have wine and entertain, and your available space.

Sparkling Wines: French Champagnes and California sparkling wines complement some of the most difficult dishes for pairing, like those high in salt, heavy cream, and fried foods. Also, sparkling wines are good to have at hand for an impromptu celebration.

Sauvignon Blanc or Riesling: For riesling, look for appellations in Washington and New York. These white wines contain bright fruit and usually moderate alcohol, which together work well when paired with salads and vegetarian dishes. A good, dry riesling is always a pleasant surprise for guests who have grown tired of chardonnay. Add chardonnay to this category if you wish—it works well as an apéritif. For sauvignon blanc, look for appellations in New Zealand, Sonoma, Washington, and Oregon.

Pinot Noir, Sangiovese or Tempranillo: While pinot noir is sometimes considered the red wine for white wine drinkers, sangiovese and tempranillo—popular Italian and Spanish grape varieties, respectively—are reds that all red wine lovers appreciate. A kiss of acidity in all three of these wines—along with moderate alcohol and minimal oak influence—helps any one of them pair with a variety of foods. For pinot noir, focus on the California appellations of Sonoma, Monterey, and Santa Barbara and Oregon's Willamette Valley. Sangiovese and tempranillo do well in warmer climates, including Paso Robles and Southern California's Temecula Valley.

Cabernet, Merlot, Malbec or Meritage: If you enjoy beef or lamb on a regular basis, any one of these wines is a must-have in a wine collection. Malbec, a blending grape in classic red Bordeaux is produced by fewer than 5% of American wineries. However, it's a major variety in Argentina, where an abundance of quality malbecs are made and sold here at affordable prices. Look for cabernet, merlot, and Meritage blends from Napa, Sonoma, and Paso Robles in California and from Washington. Merlot also does well on Eastern Long Island and the Okanagan Valley in British Columbia.

Syrah, Zinfandel or Petite Sirah: These hearty, rich, dark-fruit wines tend to have higher-than-average alcohol but, when balanced with a bold fruit component, they create nice accompaniments to grilled foods, stews, and strong firm cheeses. Look for California appellations of Napa, Sonoma, Paso Robles, Lodi, and Livermore, as well as appellations in Australia, where syrah is known as shiraz.

Dessert Wines: You may want to devote around 5% of your collection to a variety of sweet dessert wines. Dessert wines are consumed slowly, helping you slow down and savor life after a fine meal. Include in your collection Late Harvest riesling or moscato and Port-style wines.

To choose the specific wines for your collection, one way to research and identify the most popular wine producers in each of the above categories is with the help of Cellar Tracker, a huge website that collects reviews, scores, and tasting notes written by wine enthusiasts around the world. You will find all the brands capable of satisfying your personal preferences for fine wine.

Know It Like The Back of Your Hand

The exercises below concern observing wine, wine service, and wine preservation. You will compare wine legs between light and full-bodied wines, then experience the benefits of using the appropriate wine glass, serving wine at the proper temperature, and properly preserving unfinished wine:

- Compare the legs of a dry riesling that contains 11% to 12% alcohol with the legs from a chardonnay made with at least 14% alcohol. The riesling will exhibit thin, faint legs that fall back into the glass fairly quickly, while the chardonnay's legs will appear wider and take their time running back down. Taste the difference in richness between them. Legs provide a clue about the wine's style (light-body versus full-body) in advance of tasting.

- Take a typical white-wine glass with a small narrow bowl, and a red-wine glass with a wide and deep bowl, and fill only about one-third of each glass with cabernet sauvignon. Swirl them both to aerate. Sniff and taste first from the small white-wine glass and notice how little aroma and flavor you get. Then smell and taste from the red wine glass. The difference is obvious. The bigger, red-wine glass exposes a larger surface area of wine to air, which *brings more aroma out of the wine.* The shape of the bowl, curving inward at the opening, helps to contain the aroma for smelling, whereas the white-wine glass, with a smaller bowl and less wine-to-air exposure, *delivers much less of the wine's potential in in aroma and flavor.*

- Chill that bottle of cabernet sauvignon in your refrigerator for one to two hours. Then get two identical wine glasses and fill each about half way. They should feel chilled when you hold the bowl of the glass. Take one of these glasses and put it in your microwave oven—*yes, microwave oven*—and heat it for 20 seconds. That should be just enough to get the chill out and bring it to room temperature. (If it needs more warming, put it back in for 10 seconds.) Then, taste the room-temperature wine first and concentrate on *the tannin (dryness), and notice how it supports the wine.* Taste the chilled wine and notice how *tannin tastes harsh in a big red wine served too cold. The wrong serving temperature makes a good wine taste unbalanced and unpleasant.*

- Do the same comparison with two glasses of white wine. Fill each glass with either pinot grigio or riesling. Chill one glass and *warm the other for 20 seconds in the microwave* if it is not already at room temperature. Take a sip from the chilled wine first and notice its *freshness and crisp acidity.* Then taste the *flat, dull, and uninspiring* wine from the room-temperature glass. The difference is undeniable.

- This exercise demonstrates what happens when wine is exposed to air for too long and why it is important to preserve unfinished wine properly. It will train you on the smell and taste of wine gone bad. Fill one glass halfway with any red wine and place it in a corner on your kitchen counter where it won't get in the way. With the remaining wine in the bottle, re-close it with the cork and place it in the refrigerator. After three nights, take the bottle from the refrigerator, give it an hour or so to reach room temperature, and pour a glass of wine. Do a side-by-side taste comparison with the wine that was left in the glass on the kitchen counter. That wine will have lost its fruity aromas and flavors. It may even begin to show signs of sourness. The wine from the bottle that was re-closed and chilled will smell and taste fresher, more interesting, and closer to its original aroma and flavor profile.

Wine Questions Never End

As a kid growing up in New York, I just assumed every house in America had a refrigerator packed with two jugs of wine year 'round and drank wine with dinner every night. As a country, we are heading in that direction, but plain old common sense says there will never come a day when every household drinks alcohol, let alone wine.

Since 1994, wine consumption in the United States has grown every year. Think about that. In not one single year inside this span of nearly twenty years did Americans consume less wine than the previous year. Despite this growth, however, wine is not a big part of American culture. Our per capita annual consumption of a little over one case of wine is roughly only one-fifth that of France. And wine enjoys only about 17% market share out of all alcoholic beverages sold in the U.S. One question I wish I had an answer to is whether there will come a day in my lifetime when the majority of Americans who choose to consume alcohol choose wine.

And, why not? Each vintage year in wine truly does create a unique, once-in-a-lifetime beverage. Only a finite number of cases were made from that single vintage, with grapes grown under that year's unique weather patterns, by that specific producer. As the last bottle is emptied, a once-in-a-lifetime experience is gone forever.

No other beverage goes with food like wine or sends such a complex package of aroma and flavor to the palate. Few beverages have the history, mystique, and romance of wine. Even to Americans who don't drink wine, its story is both unique and provocative enough to inspire examination, if not stimulate conversation. If this book only prompts the latter, it has accomplished a lot.

Like many subjects, the more you discover about wine, the more there is to know. While each of the questions and answers in this book raise further questions and answers—which then demand even more questions—this chain ultimately stops at some that are unanswerable. Wine always was, and remains, a product of nature, created with living organisms and changeable over time. Regarding the whys and hows of the ancient and magical transformation of grapes into wine, there are some questions for which even the most experienced winemaker does not have clear answers.

Appendix 1: Know The Ground Rules

A wine appellation of origin is the geographic area where grapes for a given wine were grown. It can be a state or county, but many times it is a region within a county or one that crosses county or state borders, defined by its wine-growing characteristics. These non-political, demarcated regions are American Viticultural Areas (AVA). Different conditions apply when an AVA is identified than when a state or county appellation of origin is on a label. In addition, when a grape variety is indicated, other conditions apply. A quick-reference summary follows:

- IF the appellation of origin is a **STATE**…
  - THEN **at least 75%** of the grapes were grown in that state. Usually, multiple appellations scattered around the state were sourced for the grapes.
  - Note 1: **California** as an appellation means **100%** of the grapes originated in California. A **Texas** appellation demands 85%.

- IF the appellation of origin is a **COUNTY**…
  - THEN **75%** of the grapes must come from that county.

- IF TWO, or no more than THREE counties in the same state are the appellation…
  - THEN **100%** of the grapes must come from those counties.

- IF the appellation of origin is an approved **American Viticultural Area (AVA)**…

- THEN **85%** of the grapes must come from that AVA.

- IF an appellation of origin is named along with a **SINGLE VINEYARD**...
  - THEN **95%** of the grapes must come from that vineyard and the vineyard must be completely within the named appellation.

- IF a **GRAPE VARIETY** is on the label...
  - THEN at least **75%** of the grapes must be of that grape variety.
  - Note: Oregon wines must contain 90% of the stated grape variety, except for cabernet sauvignon-based wines, which require only 75%.

- IF a **VINTAGE** is stated on the label AND an appellation of origin is shown ...
  - THEN at least **85%** of the grapes must have been harvested in that year.

- IF a **VINTAGE** is stated on the label AND an *approved AVA* is the place of origin ...
  - THEN at least **95%** of the grapes must have been harvested in that year.

Appendix 2: Make the Most of Wine Tastings

Become familiar with different approaches to wine tasting events and outside factors that may impact your impressions of wines. Think in advance how many wines you will taste and whether or not you should apply the taste and spit method rather than swallowing wine samples. Finally, to get the most out of any wine tasting, it's important to give the wine a fair evaluation.

Preparing to taste

- Avoid wearing strong fragrances that will interfere with the wine aromas.
- Avoid eating just prior to tasting. Food flavors left on your palate will influence flavor in the wine.
- Avoid chewing gum, mints or toothpaste just prior to tasting wine.
- Do not smoke just prior to or while tasting.
- Have a white background (tablecloth) nearby for observing wine color.

Factors That Influence Your Impressions of Wines

- *Your personal preferences in wine*: If you most frequently taste and prefer big, bold, full-bodied red wines, then lighter-bodied wines may seem weak, uninteresting, and flavorless.
- *Your mood*: A sour mood will interfere with your ability to appreciate the nuances of a fine wine.

- *The immediate atmosphere*: Tasting wine inside loud, crowded rooms, or at outdoor festivals, can distract you from concentrating on and appreciating a wine.

Types of Wine Tastings

- **Vertical Tasting:** A collection of wines from different vintages that share a common feature, such as all cabernets from one producer.
- **Horizontal Tasting:** A collection of wines from the same vintage that share a common feature, such as one producer, grape variety, or appellation.
- **Blind Tasting:** A collection of wines of the same grape variety or style which does not disclose the name of the producer to the tasters.
- **Double-Blind Tasting:** A collection of wines where no information regarding grape variety, wine style, or producer is given to the tasters, except for possibly a country of origin.

Consume or Spit?

Needless to say, if consumed in significant volume, wine can have a negative effect on your reflexes, quality of work, and concentration. A winemaking staff, professional wine critics, and competition judges take a sample of wine in their mouth, hold the wine for a few seconds, and then spit it out into a separate container or sink. When tasting scores of wine in one day or in a short period of time, this is not only smart to do but required in some instances. You should practice tasting and spitting and use it when necessary to lessen the chance that your mental and physical abilities will be impaired.

Appendix 3: Store and Serve Wine at Proper Temperatures

Temperatures For Serving & Storing Wine	
Temperature Range (°F)	**Wine Styles**
65-68	Full-bodied reds, like zinfandel, syrah, petite sirah
62-65	Full-to medium-bodied reds, like cabernet sauvignon, merlot, Bordeaux, Meritage blends, Chianti
60-62	Light-to medium-bodied reds, like pinot noir, Beaujolais
50-60 (Storage)	Ideal storage temperature for all wines
57-60	Full-bodied white wines, like chardonnay
50-55	Medium-and light-bodied white wines, like sauvignon blanc, pinot grigio, viognier
46-50	Rosé wines and crisp white wines, like riesling
40-45	Sparkling wines

Appendix 4: Pair Wine With Sauces, Ethnic Dishes, & Cheeses

Suggested Wines For Pairing With Sauces, Ethnic Dishes and Cheeses

Use this table along with the Chapter 5
Food & Wine Pairing Guide
when a sauce dominates or for pairing wine
with ethnic dishes and cheeses

Sauce Base	Red Wines	White & Rosé Wines
Bernaise, Cream, White Wine, Hollandaise, Mayonnaise, Carbonara, Butter, Vinegar	Not suggested	Gets priority
Red Wine, Bean or Chili, Marinara, Tomato, Pesto, Brown Gravy	Gets priority	Not suggested
Fruit or Demi-Glaze	OK with dark color fruit base	OK with light color fruit base
Ethnic Dishes		
Chinese, Japanese, Thai	pinot noir	sauvignon blanc, pinot grigio, rosé
Greek	pinot noir, sangiovese	sauvignon blanc
Indian	pinot noir, zinfandel	chardonnay
Mexican	syrah, zinfandel	sauvignon blanc, pinot grigio
Spanish	pinot noir, sangiovese	sauvignon blanc, pinot grigio, chardonnay
Italian	pinot noir, sangiovese, merlot	pinot grigio
Cheeses		
Firm & Strong	cabernet sauvignon, merlot, zinfandel, syrah, petite sirah	rosé
Medium	pinot noir, sangiovese, merlot	chardonnay, rosé
Soft,& Mild	pinot noir, sangiovese	chardonnay, rosé

Appendix 5: Describe Wine Aromas and Flavors

Aromas, Flavors, & Other Wine Descriptors
Use the descriptors below to help identify
aromas, flavors, and textures as you taste wine

Fruity	apple, pear, apricot, peach, orange, tangerine, pineapple, coconut, melon, strawberry, plum, prune, raisin, tropical fruit, red cherry, black cherry, blackberry, blueberry, raspberry, black currant, cassis
Vegetal	bell pepper, asparagus, green olive, black olive, green bean, sweet corn
Flowery	rose, violet, jasmine, lavender, honeysuckle
Herbal	mint, tea, dill (o), tobacco (o), sage, basil, oregano, thyme, green grass bay leaf
Spicy	clove (o), cinnamon (o), vanilla (o), black pepper (o), licorice (o), nutmeg(o) ginger, exotic spice
Earthy	mushroom, truffle, minerals, tree bark (o), pine tree, rain-dampened leaves, fresh oak (o), cedar (o), fresh soil
Other	toasted bread (o), nutty (o), roasted (o), caramel (o), cocoa (o), coffee (o), jam, honey, butterscotch
Visual, Textural and other Attributes	clarity, color density, sweetness/dryness, weight on the palate, smoothness, coarseness, crispness, tartness, bitterness, astringency (tannin level), length of finish, buttery, oily, synthetic, complexity

Key: (o) = Indicates an aroma or flavor most likely contributed by oak

Appendix 6: Know True Varietal Character

True Varietal Aromas and Flavors
Popular grape varieties and their typical characteristics
on the nose and palate

Cabernet Franc	blackcurrant, raspberry, green vegetal
Cabernet Sauvignon	blackcurrant, black cherry, cedar, plum, bell pepper, tannin
Chardonnay	Apple, pear, melon, peach, pineapple, grapefruit
Merlot	plum, black cherry
Pinot Noir	floral, black cherry, cherry, raspberry, mushroom
Riesling	floral, green apple, lemon
Sauvignon Blanc	citrus, grass, herbs
Syrah	spice, pepper, plum, blackberry
Zinfandel	blackberry, black cherry, black pepper

Resources

All hyperlinks in Nose, Legs, Body! are compiled below along with other reliable wine-related resources.

Apps
Natalie MacLean: nataliemaclean.com
Local Wine Events: localwineevents.com

Books
The Wine Bible by Karen MacNeil
This book is the definitive volume on wine. It serves as a thorough reference for beginners as well as more knowledgeable wine enthusiasts.
Concise Wine Companion by Jancis Robinson
Instant definitions and explanations of terms, varietals, methods, countries
Wine Lover's Companion by Ron Herbst and Sharon Tyler Herbst
A handbook of definitions, charts, tables, maps and tips.

Wine Schools, Organizations and Certifiers
Affairs of the Vine: affairsofthevine.com
Atlanta Wine School: atlantawineschool.com
Chicago Wine School: wineschool.com
Cork Forest Conservation Alliance: corkforest.org
Hospice du Rhône: hospicedurhone.org
International Screwcap Initiative: screwcapinitiative.com
Meritage Alliance: meritagealliance.com
Organic Wine Exchange: organicwineexchange.com
Rhone Rangers: rhonerangers.org
Society of Wine Educators: societyofwineeducators.org

Wine & Spirits Education Trust: wsetglobal.com
Wine School of Philadelphia: vinology.com

Magazines

This magazine publishes "Wineology: Intelligence for the Wine Consumer" and is an excellent resource for discovering activities, events, tasting rooms, and other attractions and things to do when visiting California's Napa, Sonoma, and surrounding counties. There is also a California Central Coast edition focusing on wine regions between Santa Barbara and Monterey.
Wine Country This Week: winecountrythisweek.com

Videos

D'Anbino Wines of Paso Robles has written and produced a series of videos on wine and winemaking. This is an excellent presentation for seeing many of the steps in the process. It requires setting up with your email address but costs nothing. From Vine To Glass: fromvinetoglass.com

Vineyard Designated Wines

Dry Creek Vineyards: drycreekvineyards.com
Heitz Martha's Vineyard: heitzcellar.com
J. Lohr Winery & Vineyards: jlohr.com
Wente Vineyards: wentevineyards.com

Websites

Cellar Tracker compiles tasting notes from wine consumers around the world, providing an alternative to wine scores given by magazines and wine experts.
cellartracker.com

Glossary of Terms

Acidity: The level of natural acids in a wine that give it freshness and crispness on the palate.

Aged-on-the-lees: Dead yeast cells that settle at the bottom of a wine barrel, or tank, as the wine ages. They are manually stirred every other week while aging to mix better with the wine and create a creamy, full-bodied mouthfeel.

Alcohol content: The percentage of alcohol measured by volume (mg/liter).

American Viticultural Area (AVA): A government-approved, demarcated geographic wine-growing region whose geological and climatic conditions create wines of distinction. A specific appellation of origin.

Amontillado: A dry Fino Sherry with deep amber color and nutty flavor.

Amoroso: A rich, sweet style of Oloroso Sherry.

Appellation of Origin: A wine-growing country, state, or county.

Barbera: An Italian grape variety that produces medium-bodied red wines with a mild cherry-like flavor.

Barrel-fermented: A wine whose primary fermentation (or a portion of it) occurs in an oak barrel, typically to add body or oak aroma, or both.

Beaujolais: A sub-appellation of Burgundy, France that produces light, fresh, food-friendly red wines.

Blend: A wine made by combining two or more wines of different grape varieties.

Body: A term used to describe the weight of a wine on the palate.

Bordeaux: A wine appellation on west coast of France that produces world-class blended wines made primarily from cabernet sauvignon or merlot, or both—often from as many as five popular grape varietals from the region, including cabernet franc, petit verdot and malbec.

Botrytis: A grape fungus that shrivels grapes and concentrates sugars, producing intensely sweet wines.

Bouquet: A term for the fragrance of a wine developed after it has been aged. Sometimes used interchangeably with "aroma," which is technically the fragrance of a wine before aging.

Brix: A grape ripeness scale, used primarily in the U.S., that measures solids (sugars) inside the juice of a grape.

Bual: A full-bodied, sweet style of Madeira wine.

Burgundy: A wine-growing region of eastern France famous for wines made with pinot noir and chardonnay.

Cabernet franc: One of the classic red grapes from Bordeaux, France used to make a Bordeaux-style blend or American Meritage wine.

Cabernet sauvignon: The primary grape variety in classic red wine from Bordeaux and American Meritage wine; also the single varietal responsible for many of Napa Valley's most famous wines.

Cap: The top surface of the must, where solids accumulate and are then pushed back down (punched down) into the juice to increase skin contact.

Carbon Dioxide: One of the byproducts of fermentation. As sugar converts to alcohol, carbon dioxide (and heat) is released.

Carbonic maceration: A closed-container, anaerobic, winemaking process (without yeast inoculation) used to produce the light and fruity red wines of Beaujolais Nouveau.

Cava: Sparkling wine made in Spain.

Chablis: A lean and steely wine made from chardonnay in the Chablis sub-appellation of Burgundy.

Chardonnay: The white grape of Burgundy, France.

Charmat: A method of making sparkling wine that produces the second fermentation in tank, not bottle. Also called the "Tank Method."

Châteauneuf-du-Pape: A sub-appellation of the Southern Rhone Valley that produces a bold red wine blend using up to 13 different grape varieties. The primary grape varietal is grenache.

Chianti: A sub-appellation of Tuscany, Italy, famous for sangiovese-based red wine.

Cinsault: A red grape grown in the Rhone Valley appellation of France.

Claret: A British term for Bordeaux-style red wine.

Cold Stabilization: A step in the winemaking process that chills wine to remove tartrate crystals.

Corkage: A fee charged by restaurants to patrons who choose to bring their own wine to consume at the restaurant.

Counoise: A red grape from the Rhone Valley of France.

Cream Sherry: A dark, sweet and rich version of Sherry.

Crémant: Sparkling wine made in France, but not from the Champagne appellation.

Crush: Harvest season that starts with picking grapes and ends months later with the transfer of wine to barrel for aging.

Crusher-destemmer: A machine that separates grapes from stems and breaks open the skins to release juice. (also known as destemmer-crusher)

Cultured yeast: Manufactured yeast designed either for fermenting specific grape varieties or a specific style of wine.

Cuvée: A Champagne house's best offering, usually made from the first pressing of grapes.

Decant: The process of transferring wine from its bottle into a separate container to either remove sediment or aerate the wine.

Dessert Wine: Wine with more than 14% alcohol and noticeable sweetness.

Dosage: A high-sugar content wine added to still, base wine in order to start a second fermentation inside either a bottle or tank (from which carbon dioxide gas is captured to create bubbles in a sparkling wine).

Estate-bottled: This term indicates the wine was under the control of the producer from start to finish.

Estate-grown: This term indicates grapes were grown on the producer's own property.

Fermented in The Bottle: A term on labels of sparkling wines that indicates the traditional method (méthode champenoise) was used to make the wine.

Fermentation: The transformation of grape juice into wine as sugar plus yeast convert to alcohol and carbon dioxide (and heat).

Filtering: A process that clears wine of solids, from microscopic in size to larger visible particles.

Fining: A process that removes the most microscopic particles from wine for the purpose of clarification and stabilization.

Finish: The impression a wine leaves on the palate after swallowing or spitting.

Fino Sherry: A light, dry style of Sherry wine.

Free-run wine: The less tannic wine that flows freely into a separate tank or barrel after fermentation is complete and before leftover skins from fermentation are pressed.

Full-bodied: Wine having noticeable weight and presence on the palate. Also used to describe wines with high alcohol content.

Gamay: The grape that makes Beaujolais and Beaujolais Nouveau, from France.

Gewürztraminer: A popular white-wine grape of Germany.

Grenache: A red grape from the Rhone Valley in France.

Grenache blanc: A white grape from the Rhone Valley in France.

GSM: Abbreviation for a red wine blend made with grenache, syrah and mourvedre.

Late Harvest: Wine made from extra-ripe grapes picked late in the harvest season.

Late-Bottle Vintage (LBV): Port made from grapes grown in a single year but not in a year as good as a Vintage Port year.

Lees: Dead yeast cells from fermentation that settle at the bottom of a barrel or tank. When stirred in the wine, as done during the aging of chardonnay, lees add body and creaminess.

Legs: Streams of wine that run down the inside wall of a wine glass. Narrow, fast-moving legs generally indicate low alcohol content and light body, while wide, slow legs usually mean richness and higher alcohol.

Light-bodied: Wine that gives an impression of lightness of weight on the palate. This term typically applies to wines with low alcohol content.

Maceration: A time period that allows grape skins to make contact with grape juice, usually before fermentation begins, in order to develop deeper color in the finished wine.

Madeira: A fortified wine from the Portuguese island of Madeira that is purposely exposed to heat during the winemaking process to develop its unique flavors.

Malbec: One of the classic red grapes from Bordeaux, France that make a Bordeaux-style blend, or American Meritage wine. Also, the primary grape of Argentina.

Malmsey: The sweetest version of Madeira wine.

Malolactic Fermentation: The secondary fermentation occurring in red wine, and some white wines, that converts tart, apple-like acid into softer, milk-like acid.

Manzanilla: A delicate style of Fino Sherry that has been aged; has a slightly salty character.

Marsanne: A white grape from the Rhone Valley of France.

Medium-bodied: Wine with a weightiness on the palate that falls in between light-bodied (like the weight of water) and full-bodied (like the weight of cream). Also used to describe a wine with moderate alcohol content.

Meritage: The unique American term for a Bordeaux-style blended red wine made in the U.S. from two or more of the five classic red grapes of Bordeaux. Not more than 90% of a single grape can make up a wine labeled as Meritage.

Merlot: One of the classic red grapes from Bordeaux, France relied upon to compose a Bordeaux-style blend or American Meritage wine.

Méthode Champenoise: Also known as the traditional method of making the highest quality sparkling wine from Champagne, France. The second fermentation is done inside the bottle, as opposed to in a tank as in the Charmat (Tank) Method.

Microclimate: The climate immediately surrounding a small and precise geographic area, such as a vineyard or section of a vineyard.

MOG: Abbreviation for Material Other than Grapes, meaning leaves, rocks, debris and other items that must be removed from batches of grapes that are brought from the vineyard to the winery for processing.

Mourvedre: A red grape from the Rhone Valley of France.

Mouthfeel: The overall texture and weight of a wine on the palate, influenced by alcohol, tannin and acidity in the wine.

Muscat blanc: Aromatic white wine grape from France with dozens of variations, both in the name and grape itself. Also known as moscato or moscatel, among others.

Must: The mixture of unfermented grape juice with the solids from skins, stems and seeds of the grapes.

Natural yeast (wild yeast): A microscopic, airborne, living organism that coats grape skins and can begin the fermentation process when grape skins are broken and yeast makes contact with sugar in the juice of the grape.

Nebbiolo: A red grape from the Piedmont appellation of Northern Italy.

New World: A wine style plus winemaking philosophy and method, applied primarily to the United States, Chile, Australia, New Zealand, Argentina, and South Africa. New World wines are often made with more mechanized assistance in the vineyard than Old World wines and are typically made for earlier consumption than Old World wines. Although there are exceptions, New World wines tend to be bolder in fruit and alcohol than more refined Old World wines.

Noble Rot: A fungus also known as Botrytis that forms on grapes as they hang on the vine and causes the grapes to lose water, shrivel and become almost raisin-like. It leaves a more sugar-concentrated juice in the grapes, typically used for making high-alcohol dessert wines.

Nose: A term to describe how a wine smells, sometimes used in place of "aroma."

Old World: A wine style, plus winemaking philosophy and method, applied primarily to France, Italy, Spain, Portugal, Austria, and Germany. Old World wines are made with less mechanized assistance in the vineyard than New World wines and are typically not made for consumption young but, instead, after a period of aging. With a few exceptions, Old World wines tend to have better balance and more finesse than New World wines.

Oloroso: A rich, high-alcohol style of Sherry.

Opening up: Term used to describe the release of aromatics from a wine after exposure to oxygen for a period of time.

Pale Cream: A light-bodied, sweet style of Fino Sherry

Petit Verdot: One of the classic red grapes from Bordeaux, France that make a Bordeaux-style blend or American Meritage wine.

Petite Sirah: A red grape, also known as durif, used by some California producers to make dark, dense, full-bodied wines.

Photosynthesis: The process in which a grapevine combines sunlight, water, and carbon dioxide in the atmosphere to grow and produce sugar in the grapes.

Phylloxera: A root-destroying insect that can devastate vineyards. It was responsible for the loss of the majority of European vineyards in the late 1800s, which led to the discovery of the American rootstock's natural resistance to the disease and the grafting of European grapevines to American rootstock, still in practice today.

Pinot Gris: A white wine grape that produces a fresh and light style wine. Called pinot grigio in Italy.

Pinot Noir: Grape originating in Burgundy, France that makes delicate and aromatic red wines in France, California, Oregon, and New Zealand.

Pinotage: A grape primarily associated with South Africa. A genetic cross of pinot noir and cinsault grapes, it produces a dark, medium-to-full bodied red wine.

Pomace: The solids of skins and seeds that remain after a wine is pressed. It can be used to make grappa or brandy but is usually mixed back into the vineyard soil.

Port: A sweet, high-alcohol dessert wine from Portugal.

Press Wine: The more tannic wine that comes out of a wine press, as opposed to lighter, "free run" wine. Press wine is usually blended to free run wine, as needed, for color and tannin contribution.

Pressing: The process of mechanically squeezing wine out of the skins leftover after fermentation is complete. Pressing produces a wine of intense color and tannic structure.

Prosecco: A light sparkling wine made in Italy using the Tank Method of processing.

Pump-Over: The movement of lightly-colored, fermenting red wine from the bottom of a tank to the top in order to mix it with the cap of skins to deepen the wine's color and structure.

Punch-Down: The manual pushing down of the cap of skins at the surface of red wine fermentation in order to increase contact of juice with skins and extract more color.

Racking: The transfer of wine from one barrel or tank to another in order to clarify by separating it from sediment.

Reserve: Term used by a producer that usually indicates a wine ranked among their highest tier of quality.

Residual Sugar: The amount of sugar that remains in wine after fermentation is complete. Wines that taste dry might contain as much as 4 grams per liter of residual sugar.

Rhone: A valley in southeastern France that produces red wines made primarily from syrah and grenache, plus white wines from viognier, marsanne and roussanne.

Riesling: An aromatic white wine grape grown extensively in Germany and the Alsace region of France. Can be made into a wide range of styles, from dry to very sweet.

Rootstock: The root and lower part of a grapevine's trunk. *Vitis vinfera* grapes are usually grafted onto American rootstock for better resistance to disease.

Roussanne: A white wine grape of the Rhone Valley, in France.

Ruby Port: A sweet dessert wine from Portugal, typically the least expensive style of Port.

Saignée: The process of extracting some light-colored maceration juice either to make rosé wine or to create a more intense color in the juice left behind.

Sangiovese: A red grape grown extensively in Tuscany, Italy and the primary grape component of Chianti wine.

Sauternes: An appellation in France that produces an expensive, sweet wine of world-class distinction. Made primarily with sémillon grapes, blended with some sauvignon blanc.

Sauvignon blanc: A white wine grape from Bordeaux, France, which makes outstanding medium-body wines in California, Oregon, Washington and New Zealand.

Secondary Fermentation: A fermentation also known as malolactic fermentation that converts tart acids to soft acids.

Sediment: Residue accumulated during extended aging of a bottle of wine. Red wine sediment is formed by color pigments, tannin molecules, and tartrates. White wine can sometimes show sediment of tartrates that appear as crystals.

Sekt: Sparkling wine made in Germany.

Sémillon: A white wine grape from Bordeaux, France used to make both dry and sweet wines.

Sercial: A white grape of Portugal and a style of Madeira wine.

Sherry: A fortified dessert wine from Spain's Jerez appellation based on the palamino grape, except for PX Sherry, which is made with the pedro ximénez grape.

Shiraz: The Australian term for syrah.

Single-Vineyard (Vineyard Designated) Wine: A wine made entirely from grapes grown in one vineyard.

Sommelier: A wine expert whose knowledge and expertise is available to restaurant patrons at finer restaurants. May also choose the wines that appear on a restaurant wine list.

Sorting: The process of removing material other than grapes after freshly harvested fruit is dumped onto a conveyor and before it reaches the crusher.

Sparkling Wine: A wine that goes through two separate fermentations, the second one trapping the carbon dioxide gas (creating bubbles from an open bottle), either while still in the bottle or in a separate tank before transferring into bottle.

Spumante: Sparkling wine made in Italy.

Sulfites: Chemical compounds of sulfur that act as a preservative in wine.

Syrah: Red wine grape from the Rhone Valley in France.

Table wine: A wine with no more than 14% alcohol, by U.S. law.

Tank Method: The non-traditional method of producing sparkling wine. It is less expensive than traditional Méthode Champenoise and does not create as fine a stream of bubbles. Also known as the Tank Method because the second fermentation that captures carbon dioxide occurs in a tank instead of the bottle.

Tannin: A primary component in red wine, it is a chemical compound (phenolic) developed in wine when fermenting juice makes extended contact with skins, seeds, and stems; also added to wine as it ages in contact with oak. At an elevated level, tannin gives wine a dryness on the palate and causes the mouth to pucker (astringency), but when balanced with other components it provides the necessary structure that gives texture and grip.

Tawny Port: A style of Port wine that is a blend of different years but aged in oak for up to 40 years, as indicated on the label.

TCA: Abbreviation for Trichloroanisole, a compound that creates a musty smell in wine, sometimes caused by a faulty cork or by contaminated wood inside a winemaking facility.

Tempranillo: A red wine grape from Rioja, Spain.

Terroir: The accumulation of all conditions surrounding a grape-growing site, including soil, sunlight, daytime and nighttime temperatures, rainfall, drainage, elevation, etc., all contributing to each wine's uniqueness.

Toasted Oak: The formation of caramelized sugars in oak when it is exposed to heat, either by an open flame or oven.

True Varietal Character: The fundamental aroma and flavor profile of a grape variety that defines its style and individuality.

Verdelho: A medium-dry style of Madeira wine, and one of the white grapes that make Madeira.

Vin de Pays: A classification of French wine below the quality of controlled appellation wine (AOC) but higher than Vin de Table wine.

Vin de Table: A classification of French wine of lesser quality than Vin de Pays. It can be made from grapes sourced from anywhere in the country and with no limits on which grapes may be used.

Vineyard Block: A defined section within a vineyard differentiated by its grape variety, clone (made from a cutting from another grapevine), rootstock, elevation, irrigation or other characteristic. Grapes from vineyard blocks are usually fermented separately.

Vintage: The year in which grapes are harvested

Vintage Chart: A table that ranks the vintages from a given appellation, based on the overall quality of the wines made in each vintage. More relevant with European wines where weather influences vintages considerably more than wine regions where it is consistently good, such as California. A vintage chart may also graph a wine's future aging potential, a tool for estimating a peak time for consuming.

Vintage Port: A designation of the best quality Port wine, reserved only for years that have been declared as having superior weather.

Viognier: A white wine grape from the Rhone Valley in France.

Vitis Vinifera: The dominant species of grapes grown around the world, with its origin generally thought to be in Europe. It is the species responsible for all of the finest wines from around the world.

Wild yeast: (See Natural Yeast)

Zinfandel: A robust red wine grape that is sometimes referred to as America's grape.

Acknowledgements

Since I started a weekly newspaper column in 2001, there have been occasions over the years when people I met said, "I read your wine column!" to which I replied, "So you're the one!" To each and every reader I've met and have yet to meet, "Thank You!"

Regarding the compilation and composition of *Nose, Legs, Body!*, personal thanks first go to my wife, Kathy, for supporting me and my career change. Her encouragement and insight improved this book from cover to cover, literally.

I am grateful to the *Ventura County Star*, the first to publish my wine column, and to Chandra Grant, Editor at *Wine Country This Week*, who put it in front of millions of visitors to Napa and Sonoma. The column recently reached its tenth anniversary with the magazine, a milestone likely unnoticed by them but not me. Gratitude also goes to Mike Nordskog, publisher of *Wine & Jazz* magazine. I was honored to be its first Wine Editor from 2008 to 2011.

Chicago Wine School founder and instructor Patrick Fegan not only is a human Wikipedia of wine knowledge, he is an entertaining teacher, too. I thank him for creating his wine school and giving me the inspiration to keep studying.

My thanks also go to two winemakers who graciously reviewed the manuscript for winemaking content: Jerry De Angelis (and his wife Marsha) demonstrate their talent, skill, and passion for wine (and food!) with their own wine brand, De Angelis Wines; and

Alex Remy, a wine industry colleague and expert in winemaking technology and quality control.

Finally, thank you Diane Browning. Your perspective as a professional editor was invaluable. Your tips and suggestions worked this *Nose, Legs, Body!* into perfect shape.

About The Author

From 2003-2010, Len Napolitano appeared on *Fine Living Television* network (now Cooking Channel) giving concise advice on essential wine subjects like storage, decanting, and serving temperatures. Today, Len is immersed in wine as author, wine columnist, oak specialist, and general manager for a boutique, luxury-wine producer. He has toured the classic wine regions of Bordeaux, Burgundy and Tuscany, and regularly visits wine regions in California, Oregon and Washington, gathering wine intelligence he shares with readers.

Len's weekly wine column "Wineology: Intelligence For The Wine Consumer," ran in Southern California's *Ventura County Star* daily newspaper from 2001 to 2011. Since 2002, it has been a weekly feature in *Wine Country This Week* magazine, a visitor's guide to California's Napa Valley, Sonoma Valley, and adjacent wine regions. Len also served as Wine Editor for *Wine and Jazz* magazine from 2008 to 2011.

Len's wine study began at the Chicago Wine School and he earned certification by the Society of Wine Educators and the

Len Napolitano

Wine and Spirits Education Trust. Len also has an engineering degree and MBA in Marketing. He lives in the Paso Robles appellation in California's Central Coast wine region with his wife and two large dogs.

If you enjoyed *Nose, Legs, Body!*, a positive review will be greatly appreciated!

Read the author's answers to new wine questions at noselegsbody.com, where you can also send wine questions of your own.

Follow the author on Twitter: @wineologist.

Want to be added to the Wineology mailing list and receive news and announcements from the author? Write to: wineologist@earthlink.net.